DRAGONFLIES & DAMSELFLIES

OF THE

SOUTHWEST

DRAGONFLIES & DAMSELFLIES

OF THE

SOUTHWEST

ROBERT A. BEHRSTOCK

RIO NUEVO PUBLISHERS
TUCSON, ARIZONA

Rio Nuevo Publishers®
P.O. Box 5250, Tucson, Arizona 85703-0250
(520) 623-9558, www.rionuevo.com

Shown on the front cover (clockwise from top): Blue-ringed Dancer, Mexican
Amberwing, Neon Skimmer (bottom center and left). On page 2: Neon Skimmer;
page 5: Widow Skimmer; page 15: Black Setwing.

Library of Congress Cataloging-in-Publication Data

Behrstock, Robert A.
Dragonflies and damselflies of the southwest / Robert A. Behrstock.
    p. cm.
Includes index.
ISBN 978-1-933855-14-1
1. Dragonflies—Southwest, New—Classification. 2.
Damselflies—Southwest, New—Classification. 3. Dragonflies—Southwest,
New—Identification. 4. Damselflies—Southwest, New—Identification. I.
Title.
QL520.2.U6B44 2008
595.7'330979—dc22
                        2007048095

Design: Karen Schober, Seattle, Washington

Printed in Korea.

10 9 8 7 6 5 4 3 2 1

INTRODUCTION

· · · · · ·

The face of the dragonfly
Is practically nothing
But eyes!

—Chisoku (Japanese poet, 1640–1704)

THE FOSSIL RECORD CONTAINS EVIDENCE OF MANY ANIMALS that have completely vanished—forced into extinction by swifter predators, more nimble competitors, or climatic change. Undaunted by such threats, dragonflies have withstood the test of time. Among our most primitive insects, they belong to a mere handful of familiar creatures that may be traced to such ancient eras. Recognizable dragonfly-like insects have been found in rocks dating back some 325 million years. About 125 million years later, dragonflies remarkably similar to those we see today flew over the backs of huge, swamp-dwelling dinosaurs. Biologists refer to this form of survival as the Volkswagen Syndrome: find a body plan that works, hang onto it for as long as possible, and make whatever internal refinements are necessary to keep up with the competition. Utilizing this tactic, dragonflies have not only survived to the present but stand out among our largest, fastest, and most beautiful insects.

Modern Odonata (dragonflies and damselflies) vary greatly in size, though they hardly approach the dimensions of their ancestors. Fossil remains represent dragonflies that were nearly thirty inches from wing tip to wing tip and had a body length of more than sixteen inches. Today, the largest living species include a tropical damselfly that's just over four inches long and a Hawaiian dragonfly that's about five inches long, each with a wingspan of seven-plus inches. At the other end of the spectrum, the smallest damselflies are about ¾ inch in length and the smallest dragonfly is less than ¾ inch long.

For the past 150 years and then some, biologists from various countries have studied the Odonata of North America. Their results—published in several languages and in many scientific journals—formed the framework for classifying dragonflies; however, they were written for the museum specialist. Only during the past twenty years have North American naturalists had books for field identification of Odonata. Because identifying dragonflies in the field is a relatively new phenomenon, the field marks (visual clues that aid with separating species) for many of them are only now being developed, and it is occasionally necessary to net an individual for a closer look, after which it may be released to go on about its business.

Like birds, butterflies, and large mammals, dragonflies suddenly exploded into the public's consciousness and became "watchable" wildlife. Previously referred to by their scientific names, dragonflies became "public property"—the subjects of nature festivals and even tours to seek them in their many habitats. Now, there was a need for a set of common names that would appeal to nonprofessionals. In 1996 the Common Names Committee of the Dragonfly Society of the Americas published a list of English names for the dragonflies and damselflies found north of Mexico—a process that continues today as new species are discovered.

Classification: How Do Odonates Fit into the Scheme of Things?

Based upon body structure, all animal life has been divided into thirty-five to forty groups known as *phyla* (singular: *phylum*). The phylum Arthropoda (arthropods, Greek for "jointed foot") includes a number of well-known groups, including shrimp and crabs; spiders, scorpions, and mites; millipedes and centipedes; and insects.

Although a huge and diverse group, they are united by the presence of a layered body wall that acts much like a suit of armor. This shell or thickened skin is made of *chitin*—a naturally occurring plastic-like substance—which provides the animal with its shape, houses the internal organs and keeps them from drying out, and acts as a base for the attachment of other body parts that provide movement (legs and wings) or sense the world (eyes, antennae). This chitin shell may be soft, as in a caterpillar, or hard, as in a lobster.

Some arthropods (spiders and fleas, for example) have mouthparts designed for sucking. However, many of the living species, including dragonflies and damselflies, have chewing mouthparts. These include a pair of mandibles (often referred to as jaws), a pair of maxillae (sometimes referred to as upper jaws, in layman's terms) that manipulate food around the mouth, and the lip-like labium that holds the meal while it is being chewed. When an adult dragonfly or damselfly catches prey, it is passed from the legs to the mouth, where it is crushed by the mouthparts and then swallowed. Fortunately for us, most dragonflies are harmless to people, because our thick skin is not damaged by their tiny jaws (however, a nip from one of the larger species may draw a drop of blood).

The largest group of arthropods is the subphylum Hexapoda (Greek for "six feet")—creatures known as *insects,* one of the largest and most successful animal groups on Earth. Insects have a head, a thorax (several fused body segments that contain the muscles of the wings and legs), and an abdomen made up of a number of additional segments—ten in the case of dragonflies and damselflies. Most insects have sensory antennae, compound eyes made up of many smaller visual units, and, often, one or two pairs of wings. Astonishingly diverse, insects have been divided into thirty-two major groups known as *orders,* including, for example, the true flies, bees and ants, grasshoppers, and butterflies. One insect order is the Odonata—dragonflies and damselflies.

The term Odonata ("toothed") is derived from the Greek *odon,* or "tooth," and refers to the tooth-like structures with which the larvae capture their prey. Within the Odonata are two main suborders. These are the dragonflies or Anisoptera (Greek for "different-wing"), whose hindwings are broader than their front wings, and the usually smaller damselflies or Zygoptera (Greek for "yoke-wing"), whose hind and forewings are the same shape. Six of the seven North American families of dragonflies inhabit the Southwest, as well as all five North American families of damselflies. Each family is divided into genera (singular *genus*), small to large groups composed of similar species.

Several special characteristics separate the Odonata from other insects, including very large eyes. On dragonflies they are bulbous, covering much of the head and often meeting over the face. A damselfly's eyes are positioned on the sides of the head, separated by its face. The antennae are very tiny, barely projecting past the front of the head. Behind the head is the prothorax, a segment that bears the frontmost pair of legs. From above, it looks like the odonate's "neck." The next two fused segments are the synthorax, basically a box to which the wings as well as the middle and hind legs are attached. The synthorax also contains the large, powerful flight muscles that supply individual control to each of the four wings. Together, the prothorax and synthorax are referred to as the thorax. The dragonfly's thorax is tilted rearward, placing the wings behind the legs rather than over them. This body form may aid odonates during takeoffs and landings. It is especially useful for aerial feeders, as it brings the legs closer to the eyes and mouth. On males, note the bump below the second abdominal segment just behind the thorax. Unlike other insects with a copulatory organ at the tip of the abdomen, in dragonflies it has been displaced forward—allowing the male to clasp the female with the tip of his abdomen while he guards her "in tandem," or during copulation.

Unlike in many insects, the dragonfly's two pairs of wings are transparent and of equal length. They are built of veins that provide the wing's shape and strength, and also transport air and fluids. Between the veins are cells—transparent membranes that fill the gaps and push against air as the dragonfly moves its wings. Note that the largest veins are in the front of the wing, where they provide the rigidity needed for flight, while the rear wing has thinner veins—giving it the flexibility to bend with each upward and downward stroke. The frontmost vein on each wing is the *costa* or costal vein, which may be brightly colored. About halfway out, this vein is dented at a site called the *nodus,* where several other veins join the costa. Further toward the tip of the wing is the *stigma,* a specialized cell that may vary from roughly square to a slender rectangle. The additional weight of the stigma is said to make wing beats more efficient during very slow flight or while hovering. Additionally, the stigma is often colorful and may help species or sexes recognize one another.

Dragonfly or Damselfly?

Once people become aware of dragonflies and damselflies, they want to be able to tell them apart. These two suborders differ in a number of characteristics.

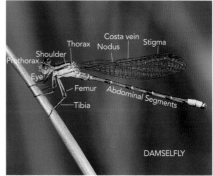

DRAGONFLIES

Perch with wings horizontal (apart)
Hindwings are broader than front wings
Head rounded, eyes often touch each other
Usually larger, more heavy-bodied
Lay eggs in water (except darners)
Three terminal abdominal appendages
Male grasps female's head during mating
Larvae have internal gills
Fly rapidly
May be seen migrating

DAMSELFLIES

Most perch with wings vertical (together)
Hindwings the same shape as front wings
Head rectangular, eyes always separated
Usually smaller, with thin body
Lay eggs in plants
Four terminal abdominal appendages
Male grasps female's thorax when mating
Larvae have three external leaf-like gills
Fly slowly
Do not migrate

Exceptions: If the specimen possesses the damselfly characteristics but holds its wings partly open, it may be a spreadwing damselfly. If the hindwings are broader, the body is stout, and the eyes are separated, it's a clubtail or petaltail dragonfly (though the latter is not found in the Southwest).

Further Hints for Identifying Dragonflies and Damselflies

Whenever possible, try to look at a dragonfly or damselfly in a systematic manner. Begin at the front end, taking note of the face color or pattern, which may have some identification value. Certain darners, for example, have a facial stripe or a spot atop the head that is a useful field mark. Skimmers' faces may be white or very colorful, or have metallic reflections; these features may distinguish them from their close cousins. The beautiful eyes of Odonata are often characteristically colored or patterned and provide additional identification clues. Note that the eyes of young individuals may be paler or very differently colored than those of the adult. On damselflies, watch for brightly colored spots or bars between their well-separated eyes. On a dragonfly, note the shape and position of its eyes, as this may allow you to quickly place it in the correct family.

Just behind the head, the prothorax may be strikingly marked. Both the thorax and abdomen of many odonates may be distinctively colored and patterned. Patterns include a variety of cross bands, lengthwise stripes, paired or single dots, rings, arrows, and a variety of L, Y, or W-shaped marks. The last several segments of the abdomen frequently provide identification clues; male clubtail dragonflies have an expanded and often distinctively colored tip to the abdomen—the *club*—that should be noted. Even the claspers, the tiny appendages at the tip of the male's abdomen, may be contrastingly colored, as they are on the sanddragons. Many damselflies have shoulder stripes, diagonal bands at the front of the thorax. Note their color, width, and whether they are forked or not. The number and position of ringed or all-black segments on a damselfly's abdomen, as well as the color and pattern at the tip of the abdomen, may provide clues as to sex and species. The legs of dragonflies can provide identification clues. These range from short to very long.

Members of the skimmer family especially have distinctively marked wings, and many can be readily identified by the location, shape, and number of dark patches, or stigmas, which may be patterned or of a contrasting color. Often, males and females have different wing patterns, allowing simple recognition of the sexes.

Male Desert Whitetail with pruinose wings and abdomen.

Dragonflies in a number of families have a pale tint to all or part of the wing or darker areas at the bases or tips of their wings. (These darker areas, often dark brown or amber, may serve to distinguish between species or sexes, and may also act as heat traps to help warm the flight muscles.)

At least six of this region's skimmers have bold, white wing patches composed of a waxy material referred to as *pruinescence*. When this material is deposited on the dragonfly's body, it acts as a structural color and appears white or blue to our eyes. Only skimmers (primarily only mature males) develop these white patches, so noting their presence or absence is very helpful when sorting out members of this family.

Life Cycles

One of the reasons dragonflies and damselflies became so successful is that they evolved to take advantage of two completely different environments during their life cycles—bridging the gap between the watery aquatic realm and that of land and air. In both, they find food and shelter. In the second, they also find mates and reproduce.

All odonates begin their lives as tiny eggs. Most dragonflies lay their eggs on the water's surface, or occasionally in wet mud at the water's edge. These may be placed rather purposefully or scattered across the surface of the water or on a mat of floating vegetation. Eggs are usually laid a few to a few dozen at a time, separating as they contact the water, although certain dragonflies known as "baskettails" deposit a ball of eggs that unrolls in the water—often across aquatic plants. Dragonfly eggs may have a sticky coating that glues them to plants as they fall through the water. A different approach is taken by damselflies and the dragonflies in the darner family, all of which lay their eggs in plants. Depending on the species, this may include rotting wood, grass stems, tree bark, water lilies, the miniature pools that form where a branch breaks off a tree, or the bases of large leaves or stems that fill with water.

Copulating Painted Damsels in a wheel

Odonate eggs begin to develop quickly, but the actual hatching time depends on the strategy that best fits each species. For example, the Wandering Glider inhabits temporary water such as rain pools. Its eggs hatch quickly, producing larvae in as few as four to five days. Other species living in more stable habitats such as lakes may have eggs that take up to several months to hatch. Certain damselflies and dragonflies pass the winter as eggs within vegetation, developing very slowly, surrounded by freezing temperatures. Such larvae can actually interrupt their development temporarily so they don't emerge while it's still too cold.

Larval damselfly, a Desert Firetail

The larvae of all southwestern Odonata live in water. Their world is a sandy or rocky stream bottom, the muck and submerged plants at the bottom of a pond or lake, or the silt of a river's quiet backwaters. Some, such as the slow-growing spiketails, may spend several years as larvae; others have multiple generations during a single year. While larvae, Odonata molt their skins from nine to fifteen times,

Larval dragonfly, a saddlebags

growing just a bit larger with each transition. Unlike butterflies and many other insects, the dragonfly's metamorphosis does not include a resting stage such as a pupa or chrysalis. Instead, when the final larval skin is shed, the adult dragonfly emerges, inflates its wings and abdomen with air and body fluids, and flies off. Newly emerged adults are ghostly pale and fly weakly until their flight muscles harden. Such individuals are easily recognized and are referred to as *tenerals*. For some species such as the abundant Familiar Bluet, the period during which adults emerge is prolonged, often throughout much of the year. Other species such as certain emeralds, spiketails, and a few skimmers fly for a very short period of time—often during early spring or in the fall. This may allow them to avoid competition with the numerous species of summer, or to specialize in certain foods.

Once adults, Odonata do not increase in size, nor do they shed their hardened skins. It is difficult to discuss the length of time various Odonata live because there are so many differences between families and geographic regions. For example, in the absence of a cold season, adults of certain tropical damselflies may live for more than eight months. In the Southwest, most damselflies probably don't live more than a week or two, while dragonflies may persist from several weeks to several months. As cooler weather approaches, most adult dragonflies die, but in areas that lack freezes, a few species may overwinter. During late summer or fall, some darners and skimmers migrate southward, probably laying their final batches of eggs and then dying.

Dragonflies in the Food Web: The Hunter and the Hunted

The Odonata are of special interest to ecologists—biologists who study the interrelationships between life forms and their environment. At every stage of their life cycle, Odonata are eating many other animals (including other insects, worms, and small fishes)—or being eaten by other animals such as birds, fishes, frogs, lizards, spiders, a few insect-catching plants, and even people. (Dragonflies—often fried or roasted—are consumed as a source of protein by people in a number of countries, either picked from vegetation, captured with sticky traps and nets, or entangled or stunned with strings rapidly whipped up and down in the insect's flight path.)

Vivid Dancer exuviae and teneral adult.

Teneral Sulphur-tipped Clubtail crawling out of the water onto a rock.

The two huge and often colorful compound eyes are perhaps the dragonfly's most striking feature. Each eye is made of thousands of individual visual units (or *ommatidia*), complete with its own lens and light-receiving cells. Not limited to light and dark, these eyes can perceive color, as well as ultraviolet and polarized light. Because of the large number of closely spaced lenses in each eye, dragonflies are especially adept at detecting motion—an important ability for an aerial predator. Note how the eyes curve around the head, allowing the dragonfly to see upwards, downwards, forward, and to the rear. If you are very close, you may see three tiny eyes, or *ocelli,* atop the head, generally assumed to be organs that measure light intensity.

The aquatic larvae may be mobile feeders, actively crawling along the bottom or through submerged plants to pursue their prey, or they may ambush the prey from a hiding place. Folded under the larva's head is a hinged lip—the *labium.* At its front are two movable jaws or *palps,* each armed with the slender claw-like teeth for which the Odonata are named. When a small creature is in range, the lip shoots forward in a fraction of a second, and the prey is seized with the palps. Prey taken this way may include various worms, crustaceans, insect larvae, tiny fishes, tadpoles, and other dragonfly larvae. In turn, larval dragonflies provide nourishment for many other forms of pond life. Even dragonfly eggs aren't safe; many are eaten by topminnows and mosquitofish, attracted as the female taps her abdomen at the water's surface.

Dragonfly Diversity and the Southwest

What do the Southwest borderlands offer to someone with an interest in Odonata? Of ten families of dragonflies found around the world, six are found in the southwestern U.S.; a seventh family—the Threadtails (Protoneuridae), a large group of colorful, tropical damselflies—reaches northern Sonora, Mexico, and it is not impossible that perhaps a powerful storm sweeping out of the Sierra Madre could conceivably carry them north of the border as well. In all, approximately two hundred species occur in the vast western region from west Texas through southern California and in northwesternmost Mexico.

Eastern Pondhawk eating Blue Dasher

Despite years of observations, we continue to learn new things about the dragonflies of the Southwest. Like birders and butterfliers, students of dragonflies have a significant opportunity to contribute to the scientific record. For example, several Mexican species were recently added to the list of odonate fauna of the Southwest U.S. Their presence here may be the result of global warming, irrigation canals and livestock ponds in formerly dry areas, or transportation by hurricanes. They were discovered by amateurs combing every available wetland for new county or state records—clear evidence that nonprofessionals can contribute to the scientific record.

SPECIES ACCOUNTS

THIS BOOK MAKES no attempt to treat the entire odonate fauna of the Southwest—some 200 species. Species emphasized are those that live closest to the U.S.–Mexico border, especially those most common and frequently seen. Also included are species unique to the borderlands of the Southwest that are found in specialized habitats, exhibit interesting behaviors, or are especially rare or attractive—species that are rarely illustrated. This book also covers several species pairs that present identification challenges.

A total length is included for each species and often includes a minimum and a maximum. Measurements of males and females are not differentiated, although occasionally there are noticeable differences. To aid with your field trips to search for dragonflies, a flight period is indicated for each species. Please note: the dates provided are early and late dates for the entire Southwest, *as recorded to date by dragonfly watchers.* Observers in Colorado, Utah, and Nevada may not see a certain species until two months or more after the earliest reported date. Our knowledge of flight seasons is based on *observer* activity as much as dragonfly activity, and every reader has the opportunity to extend our knowledge of early and late dates by keeping careful records and submitting them to a data clearinghouse such as www.odonatacentral.org.

The geographic range of a species (within the Southwest only) is indicated with the following abbreviations: west Texas (TX), New Mexico (NM), Arizona (AZ), Colorado (CO), Utah (UT), Nevada (NV), and in Mexico, the states of Chihuahua (CH), Sonora (SO), and Baja California Norte (BN).

DRAGONFLIES
· · · · · ·

DARNERS (FAMILY AESHNIDAE)

If you've spent any time outdoors, you've almost certainly seen a darner—a member of the family that includes our largest, most frequently seen dragonflies. Some species fly very close to humans and livestock, eating mosquitoes or other flies they attract or disturb. A number of darners are noticed during their migrations—passing by in vast numbers. Owing to their high visibility, these dragonflies have entered the folklore of many cultures. Their name is a contraction of several popular epithets including: "darning needle" and "Devil's darning needle"—alluding to their supposed ability to sew shut the lips of talkative youngsters.

The darners belong to a large, worldwide family with nearly 150 species in the Western Hemisphere. At least sixteen species inhabit the borderlands. Most of them belong to a colorful and confusing group of two genera that have been referred to as **mosaic darners** (the genera *Aeshna* and *Rhionaeschna*), named after the intricate patterns on their abdomens—often clues to their identity.

The darners are our only dragonflies that oviposit (lay their eggs) in plants. These include the film of algae on rocks, as well as plants that grow below the water's surface or float upon it, taller plants that grow out of the water or along the shoreline, and even rotting wood at the water's edge—an apparently primitive trait they share with the damselflies. The female's ovipositor (the modified parts at the tip of her abdomen with which she lays eggs) has tiny knife-like blades used to slice into vegetation. The eggs are placed into these cuts, safe from the mouths of various small fishes attracted to the eggs that most dragonflies scatter over the water's surface. Offsetting this higher level of parental care is the number of darners taken by bass and other predatory fishes while they pause to lay their eggs on floating vegetation. Owners of ponds are likely to find larval darners crawling about in the vegetation. Such larvae are long and slender, have widely spaced eyes, and are smooth—lacking the dorsal hooks found on other dragonfly larvae.

Common Green Darner *(Anax junius)*
FAMILY: Aeshnidae (Darners)
LENGTH: 2⅜–3⅛ inches
FLIGHT SEASON: Jan. 15–Dec. 26
DISTRIBUTION: throughout the region

Common Green Darner is the most widespread and most frequently seen large

dragonfly in the U.S. In the Southwest, it may be encountered at nearly any body of flowing or still water, including back-yard lily ponds, desert springs, cattle ponds, weedy backwaters of large rivers, and high mountain lakes. Pairs are often seen flying in tandem or perched on floating vegetation—the male guarding the female as she lays her eggs. This species often overnights in tall grasses, and an early morning stroll at a grassy lake edge may reveal their presence as they flush from your footsteps. Watch where they land and you may be rewarded with leisurely views. Note the unstriped green thorax (a characteristic of the genus throughout the Western Hemisphere) and bright blue abdomen with a jagged rosy-to-black stripe along its dorsal surface. At close range, you'll see a bull's-eye on top of the face.

This species is a familiar migrant. In the Southwest its movements are moderate. Elsewhere in the country, especially along seacoasts or lakeshores, it may appear by the tens of thousands—truly one of the spectacles of nature. During late summer or fall, both dense aggregations and thinly spread individuals moving over a broad front may be seen streaming southward—often with several species of the skimmer family—toward some unknown location. During spring and summer there are some northward movements as well, but they are less striking and even less well documented. No one has yet discovered a site in the tropics that is populated by these migrant dragonflies, unlike Monarch butterflies and many species of birds. Recent fall observations suggest that migrants from the eastern U.S. may be congregating in the lowlands of Veracruz, Mexico. Since the fall of 2005, scientists on the East Coast of the U.S. have been tracking movements of these dragonflies with miniature radio transmitters in an attempt to find out where they go.

Giant Darner (Anax walsinghami)
FAMILY: Aeshnidae (Darners)
LENGTH: 3⅞–4½ inches (male)
FLIGHT SEASON: Apr. 7–Oct. 20
DISTRIBUTION: throughout the region
   (not yet recorded in CO)

The Giant Darner is the largest dragonfly in the U.S. Like the Common Green Darner (see previous entry), it has an unmarked green thorax. Its abdomen is turquoise with a series of reddish patches. Adults fly rather slowly—often quite close to observers. If you are very lucky, you may see this impressive dragonfly hanging in vegetation. If not, males may be identified in the air with little difficulty; besides being very large, they hold their long, slender abdomens in a distinct downcurved posture. These darners occur from west Texas to inland northern California and northwestern Mexico, in habitats ranging from desert washes to oak woodlands. Although most often seen over streams, they occasionally show up at lake edges and even cattle ponds.

Blue-eyed Darner
(Rhionaeschna multicolor)

FAMILY: Aeshnidae (Darners)
LENGTH: 2⅝–2⅞ inches
FLIGHT SEASON: Feb. 23–Dec. 1
DISTRIBUTION: throughout the region

Female laying eggs

The colorful Blue-eyed Darner is a widespread western dragonfly that's especially common in the Southwest. It belongs to the group known as mosaic darners—named for their ornate abdominal patterns—which are mostly found in the northern states and Canada; three of the mosaic darners extend south into this region, and three more tropical species have established populations in the Southwest.

Blue-eyed Darners are found from sea level to the mountains, usually at reed- or cattail-lined ponds, or slower, more vegetated stretches of streams. Occasionally, one will venture to a back-yard lily pond, where a female may pause to lay eggs. At extensive habitats such as the edges of large lakes or water-treatment ponds, they may be present by the dozens or even hundreds. Even in flight, this species' glowing blue eyes will be your first clue to its identity. When one hangs off a reed, note also its pale blue face, and the dark brown thorax with slender, pale blue stripes. Above, the complexly patterned blue, black, and brown abdomen is marked with alternating pairs of large and small blue spots. The upper terminal appendages (cerci) of the male end in two slender points. The more dorsal one is longer and downcurved; together, they suggest a bottle opener. The female is similar but the blue is replaced with pale green, the terminal appendages are rounded, and she has a dark line across her face. If one is perched nearby, this line and the shape of the male's appendages may be appreciated through close-focus binoculars.

Persephone's Darner *(Aeshna persephone)*

FAMILY: Aeshnidae (Darners)
LENGTH: 2⅞–3⅛ inches
FLIGHT SEASON: July 25–Nov. 20
DISTRIBUTION: NM, AZ, CO, UT

Persephone's Darner is a mosaic darner that's restricted to the Southwest. As with many insects, its name derives from Greek mythology. As the story goes, the maiden Persephone was kidnapped by the god Hades and taken to the underworld to be its queen. Not surprisingly, her mother, Demeter, was exceedingly upset and caused the world to become infertile. In order to appease her, Persephone's father, Zeus, had the god Hermes broker a deal. Persephone was allowed to spend two-thirds of the year at the surface with her mother and one-third as Queen of the Kingdom of Hades. This darner's colorful name alludes to its inhabiting both the darker canyons and sunny hillside streams.

This rather rare species is known from a limited number of sites in northern Mexico, Arizona, and New Mexico, and even fewer in Utah and Colorado. Watch for it on small streams from upper deserts to woodlands of oaks and juniper. Should you be fortunate enough to encounter one, look at the very broad, pale greenish-yellow stripes on its thorax—wider and differently colored than those of any other species in the region. Note also the green face, blue eyes, and blue, band-like markings (formed by the fusion of the large, paired spots) on the top of the abdomen. The male's upper terminal appendages are shaped much like the blade of a canoe paddle, ending with a tiny point at the lower corner.

CLUBTAILS (FAMILY GOMPHIDAE)

The clubtails are named for the expanded tip of the male's abdomen. The family includes some of our most strikingly colored and patterned dragonflies, yet as they disappear against gravel or sun-dappled leaves, the camouflage value of these markings becomes evident. All clubtails have well-separated eyes, a primitive trait they share only with the petaltails (a family not found in the Southwest); therefore, recognizing the family is a simple matter. With few exceptions, they have clear wings; the legs may be short or very long. Egg-laying females fly about, touching the water now and then to wash off eggs accumulated at the tip of the abdomen. Once mated, females are not guarded by the males. The legs of the larvae are not as movable as in, for example, the darners or skimmers, and young clubtails burrow into the pond or stream bottom instead of roaming around. Ineffective at climbing slender plant stems as most other dragonflies do, the larvae usually climb out onto a rock or branch protruding from the water or on the sand or mud at the water's edge, and here the adults emerge.

This is a large, worldwide family with just over 100 kinds in the U.S. alone. Many are confined to certain pristine springs or river systems; their tiny ranges, specialized habitats, and short flight seasons make finding them a special challenge for dragonfly enthusiasts. About twenty-two kinds inhabit the southwestern U.S. and northwestern Mexico. Some of these are rare and poorly known; their ranges and life histories remain a mystery.

Depending on the species, clubtails perch horizontally on the ground, foliage, or a boulder surrounded by water, or they may hang from a leaf or twig. Most are found at the margins of streams or rivers, but a few inhabit lake edges. These dragonflies take large prey, and it is not unusual to see one munching on a butterfly or a dragonfly of its own size. Unlike some other dragonflies, the clubtails seem decidedly antisocial; they don't gather in aerial feeding assemblages, and the males do not guard the egg-laying females. Not only are they nonmigratory, but many species are decidedly sedentary, which, over time, helps explain their tiny ranges.

A few subgroups within this family are worth mentioning:

Named for their abdominal pattern of alternating black and white rings, the **ringtails** are a genus of about two dozen small to medium-sized clubtails, most numerous in Mexico and Central America. The word *erpeto* in the genus name (*Erpetogomphus*) is Greek for "serpent" (perhaps referring to their patterns), and indeed, nearly all of their scientific names refer to some kind of snake. Unusually attractive, they are adorned in various shades of blue, green, yellow, rust, and orange. Field identification is based upon the shape of the stripes on the thorax (occasionally absent), abdominal pattern, and coloration. Shape and size of the male's terminal abdominal appendages are the best characteristics; these can often be seen with close-focusing binoculars. Some females, especially south of the border, are very similar and provide identification challenges. Five ringtails inhabit the southwestern U.S., and several more occur in northwestern Mexico. They inhabit flowing waters ranging from tiny desert or mountain streams to large boulder-strewn rivers. Frequently, two or more species may share the same stretch of water. Mature, territorial males perch on rocks, sandbars, aquatic vegetation, and along the shore, dashing out to chase prey or engage in aerial bouts with other males. Younger males and females may be spotted nearby in weedy fields.

Found in both the Eastern and Western Hemispheres, the genus *Gomphus,* referred to as **common clubtails,** contains at least fifty species. About thirty-eight are found in the U.S.—mostly in the East. Some species are common and widespread. Others have very limited ranges—as small as a single river system—making them very susceptible to environmental threats such as pollution from mines or pulp mills. Three members reach the Southwest; each has a boldly marked black-and-yellow abdomen. The thorax is gray or olive with black stripes that may be separated by white or yellow bands. None shows the abdominal rings so characteristic of the ringtails.

The **snaketails** (genus *Ophiogomphus*) are adorned in shades of green and exhibit a well-patterned abdomen. All are stream or river specialists that demand clear water flowing over sand, gravel, or rocky bottoms. There are about twenty U.S. species, another is restricted to Mexico, and at least eight more occur in the Eastern Hemisphere. Only one U.S. species, the Arizona Snaketail, reaches the Mexican border.

The **sanddragons** (genus *Progomphus*) are large, well-patterned, tropical clubtails with members that inhabit both rivers and ponds. Of the nearly seventy species, four range northward to the U.S. A fifth in northern Sonora may one day find its way to the U.S. as well.

White-belted Ringtail
(Erpetogomphus compositus)
FAMILY: Gomphidae (Clubtails)
LENGTH: 1¾–2⅛ inches
FLIGHT SEASON: Apr. 25–Nov. 18
DISTRIBUTION: throughout the region

The White-belted Ringtail is the most widespread western member of this genus. Generally found in drier desert or scrubby habitats, it flies along open streams, rivers, and irrigation canals. The "belt" in its name refers to the glistening white vertical stripe margined in black that adorns the side of its lemon-yellow thorax. On both sexes, the abdomen shows discrete white rings and a mottled yellow-and-orange tip. These latter characteristics, and the fact that they're unlikely to hang off the ends of leaves, separate them from the Southwest members of the genus *Stylurus*, known as hanging clubtails.

Yellow-legged Ringtail
(Erpetogomphus crotalinus)
FAMILY: Gomphidae (Clubtails)
LENGTH: 1¾–1⅞ inches
FLIGHT SEASON: June 19–Sept. 30
DISTRIBUTION: NM, AZ (in the past),
    CH, SO

Although common on sunny streams in northern Chihuahua, the beautiful Yellow-legged Ringtail is the rarest U.S. member of its genus. Any sighting north of the border is a great prize, the only recent records being from two or three sites in New Mexico. Look for this species in dry country along narrow streams, where it perches on rocks, sandbars, and occasionally on vegetation. Note its unstriped apple-green thorax and yellow shins. The dorsal surface of the abdomen is mostly white, and the expanded club at the tip of the abdomen is yellow with dusky lateral marks. In binoculars, note the tips of the cerci—the upper terminal appendages.

Sulphur-tipped Clubtail *(Gomphus militaris)*
FAMILY: Gomphidae (Clubtails)
LENGTH: 1⅞–2⅒ inches
FLIGHT SEASON: May 10–Sept. 22
DISTRIBUTION: TX, NM, CO

The Sulphur-tipped Clubtail mainly inhabits the south-central U.S., where it is often common. It is named for its almost completely yellow club that is unmarked above. The face and much of the thorax are also yellow, as are thin, rearward-pointing arrows atop the male's abdomen. Each side

of the thorax appears to have two broad, black stripes that are broken through the center by yellow (front) or white (rear). The five central segments of the female's abdomen are mostly white, with black lines along the sides. Unlike many clubtails that are restricted to river edges, this species also inhabits pond and lake edges, perching on the ground or low vegetation.

Arizona Snaketail *(Ophiogomphus arizonicus)*

FAMILY: Gomphidae (Clubtails)
LENGTH: 2–2⅛ inches
FLIGHT SEASON: June 8–Oct. 8
DISTRIBUTION: NM, AZ, possibly CH

Dragonfly fanciers in the northern and eastern U.S. can practice their identification skills on a rich diversity of snaketails. Locally, only five are found in this region, four of which reach southward from their strongholds farther north or west. The Arizona Snaketail, a true southwestern specialty, occurs with certainty only in pine woodlands in eastern Arizona and southwestern New Mexico. It inhabits clear mountain streams or smaller rivers, where territorial males perch on boulders or vegetation near silt-bottomed pools. Note its nearly unmarked thorax with only a small, elongate spot in the shoulder area, followed just behind by a very narrow black streak. The face color changes with age and may shift from pale green to yellow. The eyes are pale blue to blue-green, and the mostly black abdomen is patterned above with rearward-pointing arrows of pale orange. Although this clubtail may be fairly common at a stream, the total number of streams from which it is known is small. Probably, most populations of Arizona Snaketail are on national forest land, where they receive some protection from grazing, logging, or fires that could muddy the clear waters upon which they depend.

Gray Sanddragon
(Progomphus borealis)
FAMILY: Gomphidae (Clubtails)
LENGTH: 2¼ inches
FLIGHT SEASON: Mar. 29–Nov. 16
DISTRIBUTION: throughout the region

Common Sanddragon
(Progomphus obscurus)
FAMILY: Gomphidae (Clubtails)
LENGTH: 1⅞–2 inches
FLIGHT SEASON: Apr. 12–July 24
DISTRIBUTION: TX, NM, CO

The Gray Sanddragon is found throughout the Border Southwest, where it inhabits tiny streams to large rivers. Its elevational range is noteworthy, as it flies from sea level to the higher plateaus and even along some mountain streams. Like many other clubtails, it perches prominently on boulders, as well as open or vegetated banks of sand, mud, or gravel. Throughout most of the region, this species is easily recognized by its yellow-and-black abdomen, gray sides to the thorax with one dark lateral stripe, yellow face, and pearly gray eyes.

The similar Common Sanddragon ranges westward through west Texas to eastern New Mexico, where it may occur with the Gray Sanddragon. It has a brown abdomen patterned with yellow, and the sides of the thorax are yellow with two dark bands. It has a bit more brown at the wing bases than does the Gray Sanddragon and is a bit smaller. Both species have long, yellow terminal appendages and slender spear-shaped marks atop the abdomen. Unlike the Gray Sanddragon, the Common occurs at both running water and lake edges.

SPIKETAILS (FAMILY CORDULEGASTRIDAE)

The spiketails are named for the very long ovipositor on the flexible tip of the female's abdomen. With it, she inserts her eggs into soft mud with a rapid motion likened to that of a jackhammer or sewing machine. European species have been observed repeating this egg-laying motion more than 500 times in a row. These large and colorful dragonflies, called goldenrings in Great Britain, are denizens of soft-bottomed forest streams or the riparian (streamside) corridors that line more open habitats. Instead of crawling through aquatic plants like many Odonata, the larvae of spiketails ambush their prey from concealment—hidden by sediment or bits of plant material. The larvae require permanent water, as they mature very slowly. Three or four years may be the typical larval period, but some high-elevation or high-latitude adults have emerged after seven years as larvae. Thus, a severe drought can bring a serious setback to a local population, destroying various ages of larvae that would have emerged during several different years.

Resting adults are almost always seen hanging over the edge of a stream—occasionally on a nearby shrub. Note the eyes: neither totally fused as in the darners nor completely separated as in the clubtails, but just touching at the top of the head. More often, a spiketail will be glimpsed in the air as it searches for a mate or prey during long, continuous flights over water, roads, or trails, affording the viewer little more than a tantalizingly quick look with each pass. For this reason, getting a good look at one is always a highlight of a day in the field. There are about fifty species in the family, with representatives in both the Eastern and Western Hemispheres. A number of these species breed at tiny seeps and may be the only large dragonflies in that habitat. Nine inhabit the U.S. and, like the clubtails, most occur in the East. Many species have brief flight periods, making them difficult to encounter.

Two spiketails fly in the Southwest, one occurring near sea level in coastal California, on high desert streams, and occasionally on mountain streams. The other is restricted to mountain streams or their marshy backwaters. Striking creatures, they're black and yellow with milky blue or green eyes. As is characteristic of the family, both species have two yellow stripes on the sides of the thorax and yellow bands or spots that extend down the sides of the abdomen—traits that separate them from the similarly large river cruisers. Either may be identified once the yellow pattern on the dorsal surface of the abdomen is seen well. There is little possibility of overlap, but recently, both have been recorded in the same area in the mountains of eastern Arizona, and this may occur as well in western New Mexico. Although they may spend considerable time in the air, they do alight and, with a slow approach, may be viewed or photographed at very close range as they hang from a stem at a slight angle from vertical.

Pacific Spiketail *(Cordulegaster dorsalis)*

FAMILY: Cordulegastridae (Spiketails)
LENGTH: 2¾–3⅜ inches
FLIGHT SEASON: May 15–Oct. 12
DISTRIBUTION: AZ, NM, CO, UT, NV, CA, BN

The widespread Pacific Spiketail has a greater elevational range and latitudinal range (north to Alaska) than the Apache Spiketail (see next entry). It occurs along streams in both forested and desert habitats, ranging from sea level to mountain ranges well inland. Pacific Spiketail has a line of fused, paired dorsal spots that run the length of the abdomen.

Apache Spiketail *(Cordulegaster diadema)*

FAMILY: Cordulegastridae (Spiketails)
LENGTH: 2⅞–3 ½ inches
FLIGHT SEASON: Apr. 4–Oct. 22
DISTRIBUTION: NM, UT, AZ, CH, SO

The Apache Spiketail is a southwestern specialty. Watch for it cruising over small and often densely vegetated mountain streams or muddy seeps flowing into or out of small ponds. Occasionally, they fly beats over adjacent roads and may fly right at a car's driver before skimming upward over the windshield. Unlike the previous species, the Apache's abdomen is marked with yellow rings not formed by obviously connected spots. These rings continue down the sides of the abdomen.

CRUISERS (FAMILY MACROMIIDAE)

The river cruisers and their relatives are moderately large (approximately 2¾–3¼ inches), well-marked dragonflies, several of which are difficult to identify in the field. As their name implies, males spend much of the time flying long beats back and forth over rivers and lake edges; some species also venture over fields to feed. Only infrequently will you get a prolonged view of one as it flies by, and it is the fortunate observer who finds one hanging at a perch.

These dragonflies belong to a fairly large family with about 120 species—many of which occur in southeast Asia. Nine live in the U.S., primarily in the East and Midwest. They include seven river cruisers and two smaller species collectively called brown cruisers. Two of the river cruisers inhabit the Southwest borderlands. One is largely restricted to the south-central U.S.; the other is western.

Nearly all members of this family are marked with yellow or ivory on a black, brown, or, less often, green background. The eyes are variable and may be brown, milky blue, or brilliant emerald green (the latter hinting at their relationship to the family that follows). Each species possesses a single yellow diagonal stripe on either side of the thorax; additionally, some have a similarly colored pair of stripes at the front of the thorax. Also characteristic are their very long legs and rather narrow hindwings that, like the wings of a swift or falcon, evolved for sustained flights in open habitats. In most species, the tip of the abdomen appears swollen or clubbed. The larvae of river cruisers, often referred to as "sprawlers," usually hunt by sitting motionless on the bottom. They are distinctive, being greatly flattened with a horn in the front of the eyes and, like the adults, having very long legs. River cruisers need permanent streams, as the larvae require two years to mature.

Bronzed River Cruiser *(Macromia annulata)*

FAMILY: Macromiidae (Cruisers)

LENGTH: 2⅝–2⅞ inches

FLIGHT SEASON: June 14–July 22

DISTRIBUTION: TX, NM

Aside from a single occurrence in northeast Mexico, the Bronzed River Cruiser is restricted to the south-central U.S., including Texas. In west Texas and New Mexico it is most often seen on dry-country streams; elsewhere, it flies in pine woods or scrubby woodland. Note the brown coloration and long yellow stripes at the front of the thorax, longer than in the Western River Cruiser (see next entry). The frontmost vein on each wing (the costa) is yellow in this and the next species. Where river cruisers occur with spiketails, note the river cruiser's much longer legs, single thoracic stripe, and eyes that meet broadly at the top—rather than just barely touching.

Western River Cruiser *(Macromia magnifica)*

FAMILY: Macromiidae (Cruisers)

LENGTH: 2¾–2⅞ inches

FLIGHT SEASON: Apr. 18–Sept. 12

DISTRIBUTION: AZ, UT, NV, CA (but not yet extreme southern), CH, SO

Western River Cruiser is the only truly western member of its family. It is also one of the few North American river cruisers that range northward to southern Canada. In the region, it is only infrequently recorded on rivers or larger streams in Arizona and in northwestern Mexico. Elsewhere, it is more common, occurring from the lowlands to about 4,000 feet elevation. Territorial males are most likely to be seen patrolling over water earlier in the day and feeding over land in the afternoon. Both sexes fly at various heights. Like the Bronzed River Cruiser (see previous entry), it is brown, but the stripes at the front of the thorax are much shorter. There is no known zone of overlap.

EMERALDS (FAMILY CORDULIIDAE)

The emeralds and their relatives are an intriguing family of dragonflies found in both the Eastern and Western Hemispheres. Unlike most families of Odonata, they are especially numerous from the cooler temperate regions to the Subarctic. Among them are many species that inhabit roadless areas in the far north, have extremely short flight periods, fly just after dark, or are very difficult to identify without netting; thus, despite being numerous, they are among our most poorly known dragonflies. The family is named for the metallic green eyes and bodies many of them possess; one landing on your shirt could easily be mistaken for a piece of jewelry. Although just over fifty species are found in the U.S., they are barely represented in the Southwest. Only three closely approach the Mexican border, mainly in west Texas and New Mexico. About four more range southward into the northern portion of the region.

Dot-winged Baskettail
(Epitheca petechialis)
FAMILY: Corduliidae (Emeralds)
LENGTH: 1⅜–1¾ inches
FLIGHT SEASON: Mar. 23–July 29
DISTRIBUTION: TX, NM, CO

The baskettails are mostly small and rather drab brown dragonflies. Their abdomens are spindle-shaped—that is, broad in the middle and pointed front and rear. Some have green eyes, but their bodies lack the extensive metallic green coloration of their northern cousins. A few have colored bands, tinted areas, or triangular spots in their wings, or patterns of tiny dots. Unfortunately, these patterns are variable and not always of use for field identification. Like some skimmers, baskettails have yellow bands on the thorax and a row of yellow dashes along the sides of the abdomen. They may be seen clinging horizontally to a stem or hanging from a perch. There are nine or ten baskettail species in North America; two are restricted to the northern states and two to the Southeast. The only large member of the genus is the darner-sized Prince Baskettail, which is only a very rare visitor to the area covered in this book; it differs as well in having a series of large, dark brown bands the length of its wings. The name baskettail refers to the female's habit of forming a ball of hundreds of eggs on the tip of her abdomen, depositing all of these at once. When the ball is placed in the water, it unrolls into a string of eggs and sinks, often settling on submerged aquatic vegetation.

Baskettails inhabit pond and lake edges and the quiet backwaters of rivers. They also may be encountered in marshes, meadows, weedy fields, patrolling over roads, or roosting at woodland edges. Some species are decidedly scarce, while others occur in large numbers. Males patrol back and forth at the edge of the water, pausing occasionally to hover.

SKIMMERS (FAMILY LIBELLULIDAE)

My guess is that your introduction to the world of dragonflies will begin with a skimmer—our commonest and most frequently encountered dragonflies. Skimmers range from tiny to large, slender to broad, reclusive to flamboyant, and dull to breathtaking. Many of our species are arrayed in colors and patterns that proclaim their identity and quite a few are some shade of red, a color generally absent in other families of dragonflies. Whatever their size, color, or pattern, all members of the skimmer family have a distinctive group of cells in the hindwing that resembles a downward-pointing foot, complete with a heel and toe. This group of cells is referred to as the anal loop, and only in skimmers is it foot-shaped.

Members of the largest family of dragonflies, skimmers are found everywhere but the Antarctic. In the U.S., their diversity is similar to that of the clubtails, with just over 100 species. Unlike the clubtails, however, the skimmers are more common at standing water such as lakes or ponds, more widespread, less dependent on unspoiled rivers, and more likely to be seen by the casual observer. Some species, including the large, brightly colored Flame Skimmer, are attracted to back-yard ponds, where their egg-laying, emergence, and adult behaviors are readily observed. Many skimmers are habitat "generalists" and find their way to less-than-pristine waters, including mineralized lakes and even the rich, organic waters of sewage-treatment facilities and livestock ponds.

Skimmers are well represented in the Southwest, where at least sixty-five species—about a third of the region's entire odonate fauna—may be encountered. This total includes about ten northerly pond species—members of the **whitefaces** (genus *Leucorhinia*) and **meadowhawks** that have a minor presence in the region. Both of these range southward into Nevada, Utah, and Colorado (rarely northern Arizona or northern New Mexico) from their strongholds in the northern U.S. and southern Canada. A few meadowhawks range farther southward into Mexico. The total of sixty-five Southwest skimmers also includes at least four species known from northern Chihuahua and Sonora but not yet documented north of the border.

Most skimmers are readily identified by their striking colors, body patterns, and, in some, their distinctively marked wings. Mature males are usually more brightly colored than the females, often sporting white wing patches—the only family of dragonflies to do so. Males of many skimmers guard the females as they lay their eggs, either flying along with them in tandem (contact guarding) or flying just over them (hover guarding). Most species perch horizontally on branch tips, the arcing stems of water plants, or occasionally on the ground; however, some of the **gliders** and the **clubskimmers** hang from vegetation. Males of a few species form large, aerial feeding parties, sometimes numbering in the hundreds. A few, most notably the **saddlebags** and **rainpool gliders,** are well-known migrants.

Among the skimmers, the **setwings** (genus *Dythemis*) are seven medium-sized, usually slender dragonflies that perch horizontally with a characteristic droop-winged posture. On all setwings, the wings and legs appear proportionally longer than in many other genera of skimmers. Some species are clear-winged; others have tinted veins or large hindwing patches. Females and some males may have darkened wing tips. Four species inhabit the American Southwest, from west Texas to southern Arizona; two more live in Sonora but are unlikely to cross the border. In the region, Black and Checkered Setwings are probably the most likely to be encountered. Mature males can be identified with confidence, but immatures and females present certain challenges. The three species covered in this book illustrate the variability within the genus.

The **dragonlets** (genus *Erythrodiplax*) are a genus of nearly sixty small to tiny (approximately one inch) dragonflies that inhabit pond and stream edges, meadows and weedy fields, rain pools, marshes, woodland trails, and sluggish canals. Most occur in the tropics, but five have reached the Southwest, including northwest Mexico. Many are colorful, and a number of the tropical species are red. Additionally, some have ornate patches at the base or center of the wings. Males of the southwestern species are blue or black; the females are usually brown or yellow.

Eleven members of the genera *Libellula* and *Plathemis*, sometimes referred to as **king skimmers,** inhabit the region. Because they are colorful, abundant, and easily seen, they—perhaps more than any other Odonata—come to mind when the word "dragonfly" is mentioned. Of the southwestern species, four are widespread and seven are largely western. Noting the distinctive wing patterns, as well as the presence or absence of white wing patches in mature males, will aid identification. The gaudy Flame Skimmer is probably the most frequently seen Southwest species, occurring on a wide variety of wetlands and at many elevations.

The very successful genus *Sympetrum* includes about sixty-six dainty species that range from sea level to high mountain ponds, being absent only from Australia and Antarctica. In North America they are called **meadowhawks.** Fourteen kinds inhabit the U.S. Most occur in the northern states, often in huge numbers. Only a few reach the southern border; several more fly just a bit farther north. Their males are usually bright red; females are similarly marked but paler. A few have boldly patterned wings. Face color, thoracic spots or stripes, and small black marks on the abdomen aid recognition. To identify some, especially the confusing pale immatures, the shape of the copulatory structures on the second abdominal segment must be examined in hand. A few species have decidedly late flight periods, and any individual seen during the later part of the year should be carefully identified, as both the locally scarce Spot-winged Meadowhawk and Autumn Meadowhawk (*Sympetrum vicinum,* not considered herein) have late flight seasons.

Other members of the skimmer family include groups known as **pennants, pondhawks, amberwings, gliders,** and **saddlebags.**

Red-tailed Pennant
(Brachymesia furcata)

FAMILY: Libellulidae (Skimmers)
LENGTH: 1⅜–1¾ inches
FLIGHT SEASON: Mar. 9–Nov. 25
DISTRIBUTION: TX, AZ, CA, SO, BN
    (probably NM and CH)

Dragonflies in several genera are referred to as pennants, alluding to their habit of perching on wispy vegetation where they flutter in the breeze like flags. The Red-tailed Pennant belongs to a genus of three dissimilar species—one red, one brown, and one black, all three of which can have wings varying from almost unmarked to heavily patterned. Two, including this one, are widespread in the tropics. The third has not yet been sighted south of the U.S. border, although it very likely occurs there.

The Red-tailed Pennant inhabits large rivers, lakes (including mineralized ones), and occasionally large ornamental water features. Despite their name, they often perch on branches or the ground. Territorial males spend much time in flight but alight often enough to provide the viewer with good looks. Females and young males are often seen resting on trees or shrubs at woodland edges. Both sexes have brown eyes and an unmarked, dull brown thorax. The male has a red face and a bright red abdomen. The female's abdomen is a pale honey brown to dull red, with small amber spots at the wing bases—larger on the hindwings.

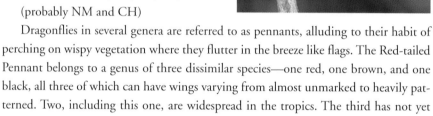

Pale-faced Clubskimmer
(Brechmorhoga mendax)

FAMILY: Libellulidae (Skimmers)
LENGTH: 2⅛–2½ inches
FLIGHT SEASON: Apr. 20–Nov. 18
DISTRIBUTION: throughout the region except CO

The clubskimmers include about fourteen difficult-to-identify dragonflies most numerous in Central and South America. Even under a microscope, their genitalia are confusingly similar. To make matters worse, they are fast, acrobatic fliers, making them hard to net for positive identification; so their ranges and flight seasons are poorly understood. They get their name from the expanded tip to the abdomen that is easily seen as they fly by, a characteristic usually associated with the clubtail family. Two inhabit the Southwest, but one is very rare and not likely to be encountered.

The Pale-faced Clubskimmer is a common, although not always easy to see, species that occurs throughout most of the region. An inhabitant of river or stream edges, it may also be seen flying along roads or woodland edges near water, often for extended periods of time. With patience, or luck, you may see one land, always hanging from a bit of vegetation. Note the striking blue-gray eyes, pale-blue-and-brown striped thorax, and the mostly slender, black abdomen marked with two elongate spots on top of segment seven.

Halloween Pennant
(Celithemis eponina)

FAMILY: Libellulidae (Skimmers)
LENGTH: 1⅜–1⅝ inches
FLIGHT SEASON: June 20–Sept. 19
DISTRIBUTION: TX, NM, CO, AZ

Members of this genus, one of several genera referred to as "pennants," perch and flutter at the tips of weeds or grass stems. This genus includes eight species; most are restricted to the eastern or southeastern U.S., but the red-and-black or yellow-and-black Calico Pennant (*Celithemis elisa,* not featured in this book) has recently been found in Colorado. All are rather small and usually red or blue. Four have patches at the hindwing bases and four have a pattern that covers most of the front and hindwings.

The beautiful Halloween Pennant is the largest and most widespread member of its clan, occurring throughout the eastern U.S. It becomes a sparse resident in west Texas, Colorado, and New Mexico, and was first recorded in southeastern Arizona during 2006. As its name implies, the colorful males have orange-tinted wings patterned with dark brown. On the similar females, the reds and oranges are replaced with yellow. More than one author has referred to this species' fluttering flight and superficial resemblance to a butterfly. Occasionally, Halloween Pennants are very common; watch for them at vegetated lake or pond edges, in marshes, or in nearby weedy fields.

Black Setwing *(Dythemis nigrescens)*

FAMILY: Libellulidae (Skimmers)
LENGTH: 1⅝–1¾ inches
FLIGHT SEASON: Apr. 23–Nov. 25
DISTRIBUTION: TX, NM, AZ, SO

The Black Setwing is blue-black, including the eyes, with a very slender abdomen. The top of the face is a bright, metallic blue. It may be found at either rivers or ponds and is often seen perched on foliage along shaded trails or at woodland edges some distance from water. Females are thicker-bodied and mainly black-patterned, with white streaks. They resemble the more easterly Swift Setwing (*Dythemis velox*, not featured in this book), which has small orange patches at the wing bases. At certain sites, Black Setwings may be very common.

Checkered Setwing *(Dythemis fugax)*

FAMILY: Libellulidae (Skimmers)
LENGTH: 1¾–2 inches
FLIGHT SEASON: May 8–Nov. 7
DISTRIBUTION: TX, NM, AZ

The Checkered Setwing is one of the most striking Southwest dragonflies. Unlike its tropical relatives, its stronghold is in the *Female*
U.S., with populations limited to Texas and several nearby states. Both sexes have a brown thorax and a black abdomen patterned above with white rectangles and triangles, and laterally with similarly colored streaks. The eyes are red above and pearly grey below, and the hindwings have *Male* orangey-brown patches at the bases. The

combination of the abdominal pattern and the large hindwing patches should cinch its identification. This species is stouter than Black Setwing (see previous entry) and, like it, may be found at streams or ponds, and occasionally on shrubs or barbed wire far from water.

Mayan Setwing *(Dythemis maya)*

FAMILY: Libellulidae (Skimmers)
LENGTH: 1⅝–1¾ inches
FLIGHT SEASON: July 27–Oct. 4
DISTRIBUTION: TX, AZ, SO (probably NM and CH)

Barely crossing the Mexican border, the beautiful Mayan Setwing is known mainly from Big Bend Ranch State Park in west Texas. Additionally, single individuals have been found at three sites in southeast Arizona. Even in Mexico it is spottily distributed. This species is usually found on streams in desert canyons but was photographed in southeast Arizona at an artificial pond in oak-juniper woodland at 5,800 feet elevation. Resembling in appearance (but not behaving like) a saddlebags, the stunning males are slender and brilliant red-orange from end to end, with similarly colored patches at the hindwing bases. There are no black marks on its abdomen. Females are orangey-brown with dark wing tips. This species may share a stem with a Flame Skimmer (see page 37); the latter is more heavily built, with orange reaching halfway out the wings. Neon Skimmer (see page 37) is similarly colored but lacks the colorful patches at the hindwing bases.

Western Pondhawk
(*Erythemis collocata*)

FAMILY: Libellulidae (Skimmers)
LENGTH: 1½–1⅝ inches
FLIGHT SEASON: Feb. 17–Nov. 25
DISTRIBUTION: throughout the region

Female

The pondhawks are a genus of ten red, blue, black, or green dragonflies, half of which have been found in the U.S. Several are among the only skimmers that habitually perch directly on the ground. One that frequently does so is the Western Pondhawk. Both the powder-blue males and the green females are often seen on trails, boat

Male

ramps, or flat vegetation such as lily pads or mats of floating algae. The green-faced adult males resemble Blue Dashers (see page 39) but lack the dasher's white face. Also, young male and female Blue Dashers have a striped thorax and a series of paired streaks along the top of the abdomen, not found on the Western Pondhawk. The male Comanche Skimmer (see page 36) is similar to the Western Pondhawk but has a white face and the wings show striking white stigmas. The female Western Pondhawk is more thickset than the male and is one of our only green dragonflies. Western Pondhawk may be encountered at streams, vegetated lake edges, or small ponds. Often a desert species in the Southwest; elsewhere it inhabits ponds along rainy seacoasts.

Great Pondhawk
(*Erythemis vesiculosa*)

FAMILY: Libellulidae (Skimmers)
LENGTH: 2¼ inches
FLIGHT SEASON: Aug. 7–Sept. 9 for
    Southwest U.S.; perhaps year-round
    in SO
DISTRIBUTION: TX, NM, AZ, SO
(continues with Pin-tailed Pondhawk, next page)

Pin-tailed Pondhawk
(Erythemis plebeja)

FAMILY: Libellulidae (Skimmers)

LENGTH: 1⅝–1⅞ inches

FLIGHT SEASON: one Sept. 9 record from
    Southwest U.S.; perhaps year-round
    in SO

DISTRIBUTION: SO, recorded once in AZ

Two other tropical pondhawks, more common in Sonora, have a minor presence in the region. Locally, both are most likely to be encountered at ponds; elsewhere, they are also found in gardens, pastures, or wooded trails near water.

Both sexes of the Great Pondhawk are emerald green with a very thin, brown- or black-banded abdomen. Abundant much farther south, it is rare from west Texas to Arizona, and in Colorado. The very different Pin-tailed Pondhawk resembles no other dragonfly in the region. Males are totally black, with a needle-like abdomen. The females are a bit stockier, with alternating light and dark brown bands on the abdomen. Like Western Pondhawk (see page 33), it often sits on the ground. It has been recorded once in Arizona. Great Pondhawk has been found during August and September, and Pin-tailed Pondhawk in September, suggesting their presence in the Southwest is related to the summer's monsoon rains.

Seaside Dragonlet
(Erythrodiplax berenice)

Female

FAMILY: Libellulidae (Skimmers)

LENGTH: 1¼–1⅜ in

FLIGHT SEASON: May 4–Oct. 2

DISTRIBUTION: TX, NM, SO, BN

Male

The dragonlets include one of the most unusual of all Odonata, the diminutive Seaside Dragonlet, the only true saltwater dragonfly in the Americas. This species ranges from northeastern Canada along the Atlantic and Gulf of Mexico to the coasts of Venezuela and Trinidad. Rarely is it found more than a few hundred yards from the immediate coast. However, there are disjunct (widely separated) populations in west Texas and New Mexico, where desert lakes provide this species' salty or mineralized habitat. As well, it is found in salt marshes along both coasts of the Gulf of California. Adult males are black; younger males and females are patterned in black and bright yellow. Where abundant (and they often are) they attract predators such as shorebirds, herons, flycatchers, and sparrows.

Plateau Dragonlet
(Erythrodiplax basifusca)

FAMILY: Libellulidae (Skimmers)

LENGTH: 1–1⅛ inches

FLIGHT SEASON: Mar. 11–Nov. 18

DISTRIBUTION: TX, NM, AZ, CA, CH, SO, BN

Female

The tiny Plateau Dragonlet is widespread in the Southwest, where it is found at stream and pond edges from central Texas to Arizona, California (rarely), and northwest Mexico. Males are easily recognized by their small size and their black head and thorax contrasting with a pale blue, black-tipped abdomen. Females and

Male

immatures are dull yellow with no really characteristic markings. Fortunately, in the Southwest, they aren't likely to overlap with any very similar species.

Black-winged Dragonlet
(Erythrodiplax funerea)

FAMILY: Libellulidae (Skimmers)

LENGTH: 1½–1⅞ inches

FLIGHT SEASON: July 18–Oct. 11

DISTRIBUTION: TX (central), AZ, SO

Although abundant in the tropics south to Ecuador, the Black-winged Dragonlet is among the rarest U.S. dragonflies. In the region, it has been recorded once in Arizona, and at just a few sites in Sonora. The dainty males are black with long, solid black patches that cover much of each wing. Females are brown and may have a dusky suffusion in the wing. Individuals will perch solidly on branches or atop a fine weed or grass stem, fluttering like a pennant. Unlike most dragonflies, perched individuals often hold their front and hindwings at different levels, making them resemble a tiny biplane. In Sonora, this species is found at streams, weedy irrigation ditches, ponds, and marshy areas. Recent reports of Black-winged Dragonlet in the Southwest have turned out to be the confusingly similar Filigree Skimmer (see page 44), another species whose males exhibit extensive black in the wings. Note the Filigree Skimmer's habit of often sitting on a rock or directly on the ground, as well as its brown striped eyes, whereas the dragonlet sits on foliage such as a stem and has solid dark eyes.

Comanche Skimmer
(Libellula comanche)

Female

FAMILY: Libellulidae (Skimmers)
LENGTH: 1⅞–2⅛ inches
FLIGHT SEASON: May 2–Nov. 1
DISTRIBUTION: throughout the region

Male

The handsome Comanche Skimmer is the region's only dragonfly with a white face and white stigmas margined with black at their outer end. The mature (pruinose) male is pale blue on the abdomen, thorax, and the very base of the hindwing. A dark stripe may be visible on the side of the thorax but may become largely obscured with pruinescence. Both sexes are dark at the wing tips. Although other pale blue species may occur in the same habitat (i.e., Blue Dasher, page 39; Western Pondhawk, page 33; and Bleached Skimmer, not discussed in this book), the white stigmas will identify this species. The female is similar, but her thorax has a brown lateral stripe broadly margined with white or pale brown; her abdomen appears dull yellowish with a narrow, black mid-dorsal stripe; and her stigmas are tan. Comanche Skimmer occurs in drier habitats at elevations from sea level to over 4,000 feet in the higher valleys and high deserts. It is a regular at desert springs and their associated marshes, and may also be common in vegetation along the slower portions of larger rivers, or perching on rushes or cattails at pond edges—both freshwater and mineralized.

Widow Skimmer *(Libellula luctuosa)*

FAMILY: Libellulidae (Skimmers)
LENGTH: 1⅜–2 inches
FLIGHT SEASON: May 5–Nov. 26
DISTRIBUTION: throughout the region
  but apparently not yet recorded in UT

A large dragonfly tastefully attired in black and white, Widow Skimmer is one of the most widespread dragonflies in the eastern U.S., continuing westward along the southern border and north along the Pacific Coast. In the Southwest, it is seen along streams with vegetated margins, at the edges of ponds and lakes, and in nearby weedy fields from sea level to over 4,000 feet elevation. Both sexes are easily recognized by the large dark brown or black patches covering the inner half of the wing. Additionally, the female's wing tips are dark. Mature males develop frosty white pruinescence that covers much of the outer half of the wings and makes their abdomen and thorax appear pale blue. Young males and females have a yellowish abdomen with a dark mid-dorsal stripe, rather like the Comanche Skimmer's (see page 36).

Flame Skimmer *(Libellula saturata)*

FAMILY: Libellulidae (Skimmers)
LENGTH: 2–2⅜ inches
FLIGHT SEASON: Feb. 9–Dec. 15
DISTRIBUTION: throughout the region

A large, brilliant flash of orange streaking across a southwestern pond will almost certainly be a Flame Skimmer. Territorial males have little tolerance for each other, and often two or even three participate in acrobatic chases, driving intruders from favored perches or away from a prospective mate. The Flame Skimmer is widespread in the western U.S., ranging from sea level to at least 6,000 feet elevation. One of our most familiar species, it may be encountered at streams, ponds, lake edges, desert oases, marshes, and (often) back-yard ornamental pools. Males have a carrot-orange body, and that color continues uniformly about halfway out the wing. Females are browner, and the orange in the wings is restricted to the forward edges, extending nearly to the wing tip.

Neon Skimmer *(Libellula croceipennis)*

FAMILY: Libellulidae (Skimmers)
LENGTH: 2⅛–2¼ inches
FLIGHT SEASON: Apr. 23–Nov. 2
DISTRIBUTION: TX, NM, UT, AZ, CA,
    BN, SO (and probably CH)

Another large, flashy dragonfly, the Neon Skimmer is similar to the Flame Skimmer (see previous entry), but males are a brighter red. The orange marks at the wing bases are not as broad, and the color is restricted to the front edge of the wings. The female's wing pattern is similar to the Flame Skimmer's, but the orange is paler. Neon Skimmer is much more a stream species; in the Southwest it is generally absent from ponds, although wanderers occasionally show up at a residential water garden. In the canyons, these may fly side-by-side—occasionally in the company of Red Rock Skimmer (which has a black pattern on the abdomen and, unlike the other two, perches on boulders; see page 40). Locally, either may occur with the rare Mayan Setwing (see page 32), a slender red-orange species with bright patches on its hindwing bases.

Four-spotted Skimmer
(*Libellula quadrimaculata*)

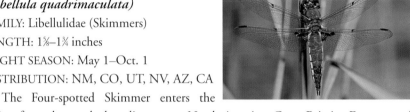

FAMILY: Libellulidae (Skimmers)
LENGTH: 1⅜–1¾ inches
FLIGHT SEASON: May 1–Oct. 1
DISTRIBUTION: NM, CO, UT, NV, AZ, CA

The Four-spotted Skimmer enters the region from the north, breeding across North America, Great Britain, Europe, and Asia. In the Eastern Hemisphere this species exhibits massive flights. Periodically, it undergoes spectacular irruptive movements; dense swarms nearly one-third of a mile long with an estimated 2.5 billion individuals have been reported. This swarming behavior may be related to the presence of internal parasites. Both sexes are dull brown, with black atop the last several abdominal segments. There are yellow dashes along the sides of the abdominal segments, yellow lines along the front of each wing, and often two yellow spots low on the side of the thorax. The four spots for which this species is named are the dark spots midway out each wing at the nodus; additionally, the hindwings each have a dark triangle at the base. Were it not for its very broad-based abdomen and its habit of perching prominently at the water's edge instead of frenetically patrolling, it might be mistaken for some species of baskettail. This species is widespread in the region, generally at higher elevations. It is generally not seen near the border and has not been recorded in Mexico. However, it should be watched for throughout the Southwest, where it could occur at streams, marshes, or lake edges at almost any altitude.

Roseate Skimmer (*Orthemis ferruginea*)

FAMILY: Libellulidae (Skimmers)
LENGTH: 2–2⅛ inches
FLIGHT SEASON: Feb. 25–Jan. 25
DISTRIBUTION: throughout the region

The Roseate Skimmer belongs to a genus of nearly twenty skimmers that inhabit the

Female

American tropics. Males of many of them are a shade of red, but a few are powder blue or patterned with other colors. Females of the more northerly species are brown. Three species inhabit the U.S., of which one is widespread in the Southwest.

With its maroon thorax, unpatterned bright pink abdomen, and unpatterned wings, an adult male Roseate Skimmer is unlikely to be confused with any other Southwest dragonfly. The reddish-brown females and immature males are very differ-

Male

ent looking; note their grayish-striped thorax. Watch also the black-edged fin-like enlargements on the female's eighth abdominal segment. If you find one laying eggs, watch her scoop up a drop of water, tossing both it and the egg on shore where it will be safe, at least temporarily, from small fishes. While she is egg-laying, her mate will almost certainly be flying nearby—hover guarding—to protect her from the amorous advances of other males.

Roseate Skimmers inhabit pond and lake edges, streams, and flooded roadside ditches, occasionally showing up at ornamental water gardens and livestock ponds. They have some tolerance for mineralized water, evidenced by their presence around the Salton Sea (CA) and Bitter Lakes National Wildlife Refuge (NM). Both sexes perch on branch tips, fences, and other available vantage points. Males are more likely to be at the water's edge, whereas females, unless ready to mate, inhabit the weedy growth or woodland edge nearby. Formerly restricted to the southeastern U.S., this species is a relative newcomer to the Southwest, having expanded its range westward to California during the twentieth century.

Blue Dasher *(Pachydiplax longipennis)*
FAMILY: Libellulidae (Skimmers)
LENGTH: 1⅛–1¾ inches
FLIGHT SEASON: Feb. 30–Nov. 25
DISTRIBUTION: throughout the region
(sparse in NV, UT, CO)

Female

Blue Dasher is abundant in the East, less so in the Southwest where standing water is limited. This dainty, pale blue species is a familiar inhabitant of still waters surrounded by reeds or cattails. Watch for it at wildlife-refuge ponds, the edges of lakes created for water treatment or fishing, and even back-yard lily ponds. Territorial

Male

males take prominent perches, often on stems bent out over the water, from which they frequently dart out to chase off intruders.

The snow-white face of this species distinguishes it from the similar Western Pondhawk (see page 33) with which it frequently occurs: note the Pondhawk's bright green face and habit of perching on the ground. The similarly colored male Comanche Skimmer (see page 36) also has a white face but is much larger and has white stigmas in its wings. Blue Dasher exhibits an interesting dimorphism (two forms) not usually found in skimmers. In the eastern U.S., the thorax of mature males is boldly striped with pale yellow and brown. In western populations, these stripes, present in immature males, disappear under a coating of pale blue pruinescence the same color as the abdomen. Female Blue Dashers have a black or dark brown abdomen with short parallel stripes running down the top. Both sexes often show an amber-colored wash at the wing bases.

Red Rock Skimmer
(Paltothemis lineatipes)

FAMILY: Libellulidae (Skimmers)
LENGTH: 1⅞–2⅛ inches
FLIGHT SEASON: Mar. 16–Dec. 6
DISTRIBUTION: border states in the region, sparse in UT

At least twenty-seven southwestern skimmers have males that are red or orange. Sorting most of them out is not too difficult, especially when size, range, and habitat are taken into account. Only a few have large red or orange patches at the base of the hindwings, and among these, only the Red Rock Skimmer has very broad hindwings and a deep red abdomen intricately patterned above with black.

This species is a familiar sight to the myriad anglers, hikers, and naturalists who visit the canyon streams of the Southwest. Not only do its colorful males fly close to the water's surface, but they often perch on the trail or the face of a boulder right at one's feet—making it one of the most photographed dragonflies in the region. Unlike many skimmers, this one shuns standing water, but it may appear on boulders just where a stream joins a lake. Although absent at lower elevations, this species is flexible in its habitat requirements, flying from desert canyons to forested streams high in the mountains. The clearwinged female shares the male's black abdominal pattern but is tan instead of red.

Wandering Glider *(Pantala flavescens)*
FAMILY: Libellulidae (Skimmers)
LENGTH: 1⅞–2 inches

FLIGHT SEASON: Mar. 22–Dec. 20
DISTRIBUTION: throughout the region

Wandering Glider

Spot-winged Glider
(Pantala hymenaea)
FAMILY: Libellulidae (Skimmers)
LENGTH: 1¾–2 inches
FLIGHT SEASON: Mar. 9–Oct. 29
DISTRIBUTION: throughout the region

Wandering and Spot-winged Gliders
are referred to as "rainpool gliders" because
both habitually seek temporary water in
which to lay their eggs. The benefit to
species that lay their eggs in temporary

water is that such habitats don't often sup- *Spot-winged Glider*

port predatory fishes that threaten their eggs. Besides pools of rainwater, eggs may be
laid in irrigated fields, roadside ditches, well-watered lawns, ornamental water features
(including back-yard ponds), quiet backwaters of streams, livestock and irrigation
ponds—and even on shiny car hoods or polished marble floors that resemble pools of
water. In order to capitalize on short-lived bodies of water, these species have evolved
one of the shortest life cycles of any dragonfly—eggs may hatch in five days, with
adults flying in as little as forty-three days later. Both species produce spring migratory
populations that emerge and then fly northward, where they may produce yet another
migratory population. Elsewhere, but not in the relatively dry Southwest, these movements are large enough to be detected with radar.

The Wandering Glider is an especially aggressive egg-layer. That characteristic and
its propensity to travel have made it the most widespread dragonfly in the world,
absent only from the Antarctic. Both it and Spot-winged Glider spend much of the
day in the air, often flying together in mixed-species feeding swarms of hundreds of
individuals. With a little practice one may identify them in flight. Both have very
broad hindwings and a fairly short, carrot-shaped body—thick in the head region,
then tapering to a point. Wandering Glider is yellow to pale orange and has unmarked
wings. If you see one hanging from a stem, note the black line along the top of the
abdomen (margined with white on females), orange stigmas, and liver-red eyes. Spot-
winged's abdomen is cocoa brown with a fine dorsal pattern. Unlike Wandering
Glider, this species has small, rounded spots at the hindwing bases. When a Spot-
winged Glider flies toward you, its striking, cherry-red eyes are easily seen.

Mexican Amberwing
(Perithemis intensa)

FAMILY: Libellulidae (Skimmers)

LENGTH: 1 inch

FLIGHT SEASON: Apr. 3–Nov. 25

DISTRIBUTION: mainly near the border in NM, AZ, and CA; also NV, UT, BN, SO, CH

Female

The twelve amberwings, named for their males' tinted wings, are tiny skimmers that are most diverse in the American tropics. Nearly unique among the world's 2,500-plus dragonflies, the male amberwing performs a mating "dance," increasing his chances of copulating with a female at an attractive egg-laying site staked out by him—usually the tip of a branch or aquatic plant that projects from the water.

Male

Three amberwings reach the U.S.: the widespread Eastern Amberwing (*Perithemis tenera*) and the more local Mexican and Slough Amberwing (*P. intensa* and *domitia*), the latter not featured in this book. Mexican Amberwing, the most widespread Southwestern species, is illustrated here, but all are superficially similar. Males of all three U.S. species have patterned orange to yellow bodies and mostly unpatterned yellow or orange wings. Noting the presence or absence of stripes on the thorax, leg color, the dashes atop the abdomen, and each species' range will help sort them out. The Slough Amberwing shuns the direct sunlight favored by the other two species and is largely restricted to pond edges shaded by overhanging branches or taller shade trees. Unlike the other two species, it possesses a row of white parallel dashes atop its abdomen. Often the inner half of the female's wing is darker—a pattern not found in the other two species. Both it and Eastern Amberwing have a patterned thorax. Eastern Amberwing, the smallest of the three, has pale legs, and each pair of pale dashes atop the abdomen forms a "V." Eastern and Slough Amberwing both reach Sonora; in the U.S. they are found no farther west than extreme southeastern Arizona.

Female amberwings have browner bodies and mostly clear wings with various darker markings that aid in identification. Many observers have noted that these tiny dragonflies with patterned wings resemble wasps of the family Vespidae. Researchers in Finland learned that a darner they studied avoided not only wasps, but also harmless flies they painted to resemble wasps. Thus the wasp pattern of female amberwings may confer some degree of protection from predators, including other odonates and, perhaps more importantly, birds.

The Mexican Amberwing occurs from southwestern New Mexico to southern California and southern Nevada, and ranges south into Mexico. It is widespread from sea level to several thousand feet in elevation but does not occur in the high mountains or in dense forests. Watch for them on vegetation at pond and lake edges or the slower backwaters of streams. Like other amberwings, they'll occasionally sit atop shrubs or weedy growth some distance from water. Unlike Eastern and Slough Amberwing, Mexican Amberwing lacks well-defined spots or stripes on the side of the thorax. The females have darker bands of orange and black that cross the wings partway.

Common Whitetail *(Plathemis lydia)*
FAMILY: Libellulidae (Skimmers)
LENGTH: 1⅝–1⅞ inches
FLIGHT SEASON: Mar. 30–Nov. 4
DISTRIBUTION: throughout most of the
region (not yet recorded in UT, CH, BN)

Female

Two species of whitetails, so named because of the adult male's pruinose bluish to white abdomen, are found in the Southwest. Like many of the king skimmers (*Libellula*) with which they were formerly included, the whitetails have strongly patterned wings that aid in the identification of both sexes. This is especially useful before the males develop their distinctive, frosted appearance. Common Whitetail is widespread throughout the East and the western coastal states. It can be numerous at both moving and still water, where territorial males are involved in seemingly constant aerial chases. Both sexes perch close to the ground, occasionally far from water—often landing prominently on trails, rocks, or stumps, where they are easily seen. Females and young males are brown with pale streaks on the sides of the abdominal segments. Males of all ages have a small black patch at the base of the wings and a large black rectangle mid-wing. On females, the large patch is replaced by smaller ones mid-wing and at the wing tip. Unlike the next species, the male's wing bases are clear.

Desert Whitetail *(Plathemis subornata)*
FAMILY: Libellulidae (Skimmers)
LENGTH: 1½–2 inches
FLIGHT SEASON: Apr. 2–Nov. 2
DISTRIBUTION: throughout the region
(not yet recorded in BN)

Female

The Desert Whitetail is more a Southwest specialty than the Common Whitetail. It occurs in arid, open lowland to plateau areas at habitats such as cattle ponds, mineralized pools, desert streams, spring-fed marshes, and occasionally at lake edges. Males differ from male Common Whitetails in having extensively white wing bases. Females lack the Common Whitetail's dark wing tips. Both sexes have a broad jagged line about halfway out the wing (at the nodus) and another about three-quarters of the way toward the wing tip. On males, the space between these lines darkens.

Male

Filigree Skimmer
(*Pseudoleon superbus*)
FAMILY: Libellulidae (Skimmers)
LENGTH: 1½–1¾ inches
FLIGHT SEASON: Feb. 12–Nov. 18
DISTRIBUTION: widespread near border;
    so far only one CA record and none in
    CO, UT, NV

Many Odonata have males that are more colorful or more strikingly patterned than their respective females. The Filigree Skimmer is an exception, the female being equally attractive and frequently more so. Despite being adorned with a limited palette of black and browns, a unique, lacy wing pattern makes her one of the most attractive Southwest dragonflies. The male's wings are variable, ranging from a darker version of the female's to having long, black patches that cover much of the wing surface. The female's forewing bases are largely clear, as are the male's (unlike the black bases of the otherwise similar male Black-winged Dragonlet, page 35). On both sexes, the abdomen is dark brown, patterned above with a row of pale, forward-pointing V-shaped marks. With close-focus binoculars, note the unusual eyes. Patterned with vertical bands of tan and dark brown, they look surprisingly like polished gemstones. Locally, Filigree Skimmers are most often found in arid hills, flying on open rocky slopes and streambeds, larger rivers, and occasionally at ponds. Elsewhere they may be found in more lush habitats and at lower elevations. This species frequently perches on rocks or the ground, often with its wings depressed.

Variegated Meadowhawk (*Sympetrum corruptum*)
FAMILY: Libellulidae (Skimmers)
LENGTH: 1½–1⅞ inches
FLIGHT SEASON: throughout the year
DISTRIBUTION: throughout the region

Variegated Meadowhawk is the country's most widespread member of its genus, one of the most common, and—other than the unique Black Meadowhawk (*Sympetrum danae*, not featured in this book)— the easiest to identify. Both the rosy-red males and the yellow or brown females and

immature males have a distinctive line of white spots outlined in black along the sides of the abdomen. The female has yellow stripes on her thorax; the male's stripes are pale, becoming brighter yellow at the bottom. In the Southwest, this species may be especially common at the edges of ponds, lakes (including mineralized ones), and irrigation canals. They also show up at small streams and even weedy fields within urban areas. A stroll along a grassy lake edge may send up hundreds of newly emerged tenerals, indicating both their great numbers and the narrow window of time during which they emerge. Some western populations of this species are migratory, and movements of thousands of individuals have been reported. The durable Variegated Meadowhawk has one of the longest flight periods of any North American dragonfly—some fly all winter; on any given day there are Variegated Meadowhawks on the wing somewhere in the U.S.

Spot-winged Meadowhawk (*Sympetrum signiferum*)
FAMILY: Libellulidae (Skimmers)
LENGTH: 1¼–1⅝ inches
FLIGHT SEASON: Aug. 2–Nov. 28
DISTRIBUTION: AZ, SO, CH; almost
    certainly in southern NM

Barely entering the U.S. in southeast Arizona, Spot-winged Meadowhawk is a northwest Mexico species with an unusual late-summer/fall flight season. It inhabits mountain streams and artificial canals, as well as the grassy or weedy meadows surrounding them. In Sonora and Chihuahua, it occurs at streams in both woodlands and open areas, and may be locally abundant. Males are cherry red; the females become dull red when mature. Immatures of both sexes are dull yellow. There is a blackish spot on the rear portion of all but the first two and last three abdominal segments. On both sexes, note the patches of amber, brown, and black at the base of each hindwing. Both sexes lack yellow spots on the side of the thorax, a characteristic of Cardinal Meadowhawk (*Sympetrum illotum*, not featured in this book), with which it may occur. Unlike the Variegated Meadowhawk (see previous entry), which often perches on the ground, Spot-winged behaves like some of the pennants and is likely to be found balancing on the tips of weeds or grasses.

Red Saddlebags *(Tramea onusta)*
FAMILY: Libellulidae (Skimmers)
LENGTH: 1⅝–1⅞ inches
FLIGHT SEASON: Jan. 1–Nov. 18
DISTRIBUTION: throughout the region

Black Saddlebags *(Tramea lacerata)*
FAMILY: Libellulidae (Skimmers)
LENGTH: 2–2⅛ inches
FLIGHT SEASON: Mar. 30–Nov. 12
DISTRIBUTION: throughout the region

The saddlebags are a genus of twenty-two medium to large, well-marked species that occur in both the Eastern and Western Hemispheres. A number of them are migratory, as suggested by their very broad hindwings. During their movements, hundreds may be seen, often in the company of other migratory skimmers or darners, flying not far above the ground (where many collide with vehicles). Most species are red, although a few are black. Females are similar to males but are duller. Both sexes possess broad or narrow colored patches at the base of their hindwings—the "saddlebags" for which they are named. Of the seven U.S. species, five reach the Southwest—two of them only marginally so in west Texas.

Red and Black Saddlebags are familiar Southwest species, seen most frequently at lake edges and ponds. Both spend much of the day in flight, but watch for them hanging in vegetation near the water, or perched on the tips of tall weeds or shrubs in weedy fields. By late morning, males and females are often seen flying in tandem—the male protecting the female from the sexual advances of other males. These united pairs almost seem to bounce along the water's surface, the male holding her with his terminal appendages then releasing her briefly as she deposits her eggs in the water.

The Black Saddlebags is easily recognized—our only large, slender, black dragonfly with black patches that occupy the inner ¼ of the hindwing. The similar Marl Pennant *(Macrodiplax balteata,* not covered in this book) is smaller, has tiny black wing patches, and is often found at mineralized water. Red Saddlebags are deep red (males) or brown (females) with large hindwing patches. Both sexes show black on top of the rearmost abdominal segments. The very similar Carolina Saddlebags *(Tramea carolina)* does not occur in the region. The Striped Saddlebags *(Tramea calverti),* a rare tropical visitor to northern Sonora, Arizona, and southern California, may become locally common at weedy lake margins during favorable years, and breeding within the region has been suspected. To find one, look for a red (males) or brown (females) saddlebags with two gray stripes on the side of the thorax and narrow bands at the hindwing bases.

DAMSELFLIES

· · · · · ·

JEWELWINGS (FAMILY CALOPTERYGIDAE)

From the Greek words *callos* (beauty) and *pteryx* (wing), the family Calopterygidae includes some of the world's most beautiful insects. They have been called broad-winged damselflies because their wings do not become narrow (petiolate) at the base like those of most other damsels. These glittering species are among our most attractive Odonata; indeed, when the U.S. Postal Service introduced a sheet of spider and insect stamps in 1999, the only odonate depicted was the Ebony Jewelwing, an eastern member of this family that possesses velvety black wings and an iridescent green body.

Jewelwings are found throughout much of the world, although absent in Australia and New Zealand. They are especially well represented in the tropics, but many species inhabit temperate regions. Most have a metallic red, green, or blue body, generally sporting wings patterned with red, green, blue, or black. Large, colorful, and often perched in the open, they are a favorite of nature photographers. Additionally, many species have complicated mating postures and courtship displays and are of great interest to students of animal behavior.

Locally, the jewelwings are represented by three kinds of rubyspots, one of which, the dark-winged Smoky Rubyspot (*Hetaerina titia*, not discussed herein), is rare in the extreme eastern portion of the region. The northernmost members of a large tropical genus, rubyspots inhabit flowing waters, including rushing mountain rivers, sunny desert washes, and even tiny streams in deeply shaded Amazon rain forests. Here mature males defend their territories, from rocks, branches, or grassy vegetation. The name "rubyspot" refers to the brilliant red wing bases exhibited by most members of the genus, and several males sparkling in the air together during a territorial dispute is an unforgettable sight.

American Rubyspot *(Hetaerina americana)*
FAMILY: Calopterygidae (Jewelwings)
LENGTH: 1½–1¾ inches

FLIGHT SEASON: Jan. 10–Dec. 29
DISTRIBUTION: throughout the region

The widespread American Rubyspot is found in much of the U.S. from the Atlantic to the Pacific. In the Southwest, it is a characteristic species of river and stream edges, occurring from about sea level to over 5,000 feet elevation. Where present, dozens may be seen perching on willow stems or rushes that bend over the water. Adult males possess a metallic red thorax and dark abdomen that may appear black, brown, or metallic green. The deep red spots at the wing bases vary from about one-third to nearly one-half of the wing length. On the closed wings the patches are dull red from below and overlaid with a snowy white pattern of tiny veins. From above, the wing bases are a shocking red, and it's tempting to nudge them into changing perches in order to view that color again and again. The paler female's thorax is tan with broad bands of metallic green and brown. There is only a light wash of pink or orange at the wing bases, and her abdomen is considerably thicker than the male's.

Canyon Rubyspot
(Hetaerina vulnerata)
FAMILY: Calopterygidae (Jewelwings)
LENGTH: 1⅜–1¾ inches
FLIGHT SEASON: Mar. 18–Nov. 16.
DISTRIBUTION: TX (observed centrally,
also likely in west TX), NM, AZ, UT, NV, SO, CH

Female

In the higher canyons of the Southwest where oaks, sycamores, and pines shade the streams, the American Rubyspot (see previous entry) is replaced by the Canyon Rubyspot; only occasionally are both found together. The two species are very similar, but Canyon usually has smaller red patches at the wing bases and generally lacks stigmas at the wing tips. The thorax of the female is tan with metallic green markings that are smaller than those of American Rubyspot. Males perch on sunny boulders or branches near a stream; females are more likely to be found on vegetation. This species is not common, rarely occurring by the dozens like its lowland cousin. If you use a hand lens, males of these two rubyspots may be reliably differentiated if you look at their terminal appendages. On the American, the inner curve of the cerci has one or two prominent, tooth-like lobes; these are absent on the Canyon, which has, instead, a curved shelf on the inner surface of the appendage.

SPREADWING DAMSELS (FAMILY LESTIDAE)

Spreadwings are relatively large damselflies, with some species approaching more than three inches in length. They are named for their habit of perching at an angle on the sides of stems with their wings spread partly open. Subtly beautiful, most have bright blue eyes, and many have metallic green or blue areas on the thorax. Twenty species inhabit the U.S., about half of which occur in the Southwest. The large spreadwings inhabit streamsides, but the majority live along grassy pond or lake edges, occasionally in huge numbers. Like many Odonata, they can be found away from water and may be common in woodland understory. The family is found everywhere but the Antarctic, in habitats ranging from pools on a tropical savannah to sedge-lined ponds of the Subarctic.

North of Mexico, many spreadwings reproduce late in the year, and, unlike most U.S. damselflies, they overwinter as eggs or minute larvae inside vegetation ranging from weedy growth at pond edges to fairly stout woody branches over ponds or stream channels. Here, they sit for months, leaving the foliage the next spring to become mobile aquatic predators. Because pond edges may remain moist and green during times of drought and are attractive to cattle, livestock grazing and physical damage from being trampled are special threats to damselfly eggs that overwinter in pond-edge vegetation.

At least six species of the smaller *Lestes* spreadwings inhabit the region; four are more characteristic of the eastern or northern U.S. Most are found at the grassy margins of ponds rather than at flowing water. Some are strikingly patterned or marked with various metallic hues that aid in their identification; others are confusingly similar, and their caudal appendages must be examined in hand to confirm identification.

Great Spreadwing *(Archilestes grandis)*
FAMILY: Lestidae (Spreadwings)
LENGTH: 1⅝–2⅜ inches
FLIGHT SEASON: Mar.–Jan. 14
DISTRIBUTION: throughout the region
    (not known from BN)

Female

The largest damselfly in the U.S., Great Spreadwing is found across the country, absent only from the northernmost states. Like most members of its genus, it is more likely to be found along streams than at ponds. Originally a southwestern species, during the twentieth century it spread to the northeastern U.S. In the Southwest, it is often encountered in vegetation lining narrow, shady canyon streams but also occurs in more open habitats such as the vegetated edges of desert oases, willow thickets bordering the backwaters of larger rivers, and even aquatic-plant nurseries. Inhabiting a broad elevational range, it occurs from near sea level to over 6,000 feet. At times, it is found with the similar California Spreadwing (*Archilestes californicus*, not featured in this book); the thorax of the California is whiter, with a narrow dark rectangle on its side, and lacks the Great Spreadwing's broad lateral yellow stripe. Both of these are longer and more heavily built than the numerous smaller spreadwings in the genus *Lestes*.

Male

Emerald Spreadwing *(Lestes dryas)*
FAMILY: Lestidae (Spreadwings)
LENGTH: 1¼–1½ inches
FLIGHT SEASON: Apr. 22–Oct. 2
DISTRIBUTION: NM, AZ, CO, UT, NV, CA

Emerald Spreadwing is a beautiful damselfly with an exceptional range. It is the only spreadwing with a Holarctic distribution; that is, it breeds across North America and from Spain and England through Europe and Asia to Japan. In North America, it inhabits the northern tier of states as far as the Subarctic regions of Canada and Alaska. Although common in the lowlands in other parts of its range, in the northern portions of New Mexico and Arizona, and in southern California, it is found at the margins of ponds up to about 8,000 feet in elevation.

The larvae of Emerald Spreadwing swim about in the water and are easy prey for fish. Therefore, they are often found most abundantly at small bodies of water (including salty or mineralized pools and rain-filled ponds) that may dry out and become unsuitable for predatory fishes. Males of this species have extensive metallic green or blue-green on the upper parts of the thorax and a dark metallic green abdomen tipped with blue. The lower thorax is bright blue, as are the eyes. The terminal abdominal appendages are distinctive; the lower pair (paraprocts) appear within the broad curve of the upper pair as two feet with the toes turned inward.

Plateau Spreadwing *(Lestes alacer)*
FAMILY: Lestidae (Spreadwings)
LENGTH: 1 3/8–1 3/4 inches
FLIGHT SEASON: Jan. 27–Nov. 8
DISTRIBUTION: TX, NM, AZ, CH, SO

One of the easiest spreadwings to iden- tify, the Plateau Spreadwing ranges from Oklahoma and the Gulf Coast of Texas to Arizona and Sonora. On both sexes, note the broad black band bordered with blue on the top center of the thorax. This species occurs at various elevations, from near sea level to pools surrounded by pines at over  6,000 feet. At times, it may be very numerous; in northern Chihuahua, hundreds of ghostly pale tenerals were observed on their maiden flight as they drifted up like smoke from the grassy edge of a high-desert pond.

POND DAMSELS (FAMILY COENAGRIONIDAE)

With 102 species, the pond damsels represent just over three-fourths of the total num- ber of U.S. damselfly species. Two genera—the dancers and the bluets—are especially well represented, each with more than thirty species. Due to their evolutionary history, the majority of the dancers (many of which are outliers of Mexican populations) are found in the western U.S., while most of the bluets are found in the East. Although many pond damsels are rather similar—blue with patterns of black—this family includes some of the most striking western odonates, including the multicolored Painted Damsel and the cherry-red Desert Firetail.

The genus *Argia*, referred to in the U.S. as **dancers**, is the largest genus of dam- selflies in the Southwest. Throughout the Americas, there are more than 100 known species, and many more are still undescribed. Thirty-one inhabit the U.S., twenty-five of which live in the Southwest. About seven of these belong to Mexico's highland fauna, reaching Arizona and New Mexico via the sky islands—outlying ranges of the Sierra Madre Occidental. These include species such as Pima, Sierra Madre, and Taras- can Dancers, whose ranges are limited to three or four counties in the U.S. Others, such as Aztec and Amethyst Dancers, are characteristic of lowland deserts. A few are very wide-ranging: Vivid Dancer, for example, also inhabits spring-fed streams in coastal forests of the Pacific Northwest, and Blue-fronted Dancer flies in the steamy swamps of Louisiana. By convention, most of the region's dancers are named after southwestern tribes. In addition to those already mentioned, others include the Comanche, Apache, Tonto, and Paiute.

With thirty-seven species, the **bluets** make up the largest genus of U.S. damselflies. Fourteen species occur in the Southwest, three just barely so. Many are found at vege- tated lake edges; others inhabit desert pools, streams, ditches, salty estuaries, high mountain ponds, and Subarctic marshes. Some species not only tolerate but are particularly common at mineralized or polluted water—especially east of the Mississippi. Most bluets are in fact blue, but some of the eastern species are red, orange, purple, or black. Of the eleven kinds that live along the Southwest border, one appears purple and black. One species of west Texas and Sonora, Mexico, is dark purple; another that reaches Colorado is brightly multicolored. The remaining southwestern species are blue with comparable black patterns, and their similarities pose identification challenges. Several, including two vexing species pairs, must be examined closely in hand to be certain of identification.

Where bluets fly alongside similarly patterned dancers, note that the dancers usually hold their wings well above the abdomen, while the bluets' are more likely to be low and tented over the abdomen. Additionally, bluets tend to feed while slowly drifting through vegetation, picking tiny insects off plants. Dancers are more likely to perch on the ground, a low rock, or twig, springing up briefly to take a prey item. The heavier-bodied female bluets resemble males but are usually tan, dull olive, or pale blue, and have more extensive black pigmentation on the top of the abdomen. Both sexes of bluets may exhibit confusing short-term color changes. As temperatures vary, both the function and position of pigment cells throughout the body may change. Even brilliant blue mature males may become a pale blue-gray when chilled.

The **forktails** are members of a very successful genus whose nearly seventy species inhabit most of the world. Their name refers to the minute forked spine projecting dorsally at the tip of the abdomen. The forktails include some of the world's smallest damselflies, and learning to find them will hone your skills as an observer. Like many damsels, forktails are weak fliers; nonetheless, several have been able to pioneer remote island groups, perhaps being dispersed by winds. Ten species inhabit the Southwest, although one eastern species barely reaches west Texas. These range in size from less than an inch to about 1½ inches. Most males have five (occasionally three) black stripes on the thorax that are usually separated by green, blue, or yellow. A few western species lack stripes, and the top of the thorax is either solid black or has four blue dots. Despite being colorful, well patterned, and often abundant, not every one may be identified with certainty with binoculars, as there are pairs of look-alike species that require in-hand examination. Adding to the difficulty, some species have females with multiple color forms whose numbers may differ between populations. Such females may be pale blue, tomato red, pale purple, olive, or brown, or resemble the adult male! Forktails are most numerous at the grassy margins of ponds or streams, but may venture out to perch on a muddy river bar or appear at a windmill tank far from apparently suitable habitat.

Black-and-white Damsel
(Apanisagrion lais)

FAMILY: Coenagrionidae (Pond Damsels)
LENGTH: 1¼–1⅜ inches
FLIGHT SEASON: Apr. 13–Nov. 12
DISTRIBUTION: AZ, CH, SO

Black-and-white Damsel, a poorly known species, is widespread in Mexico but barely enters the U.S. in southeastern Arizona. It inhabits higher elevations to about 6,000 feet, usually in small grass-edged streams or the quiet backwaters and pools of larger rivers. Most will be seen perched low or drifting inconspicuously in grassy vegetation, not often sitting in the open like so many other stream species. Adult males are unlikely to be confused with other damsels; note the mostly black thorax with thin, pale green stripes, and the long black abdomen with a frosty white tip. Females are similar in appearance but have less white on the abdomen. The orange immatures have a lightly striped thorax and are longer and slimmer than the immatures of other similar species. In hand, note the strange patch of tiny veins at the tip of the male's hindwing, a characteristic it shares with no other damselfly in the U.S. At some locations, this species may be common some years and virtually absent during others, despite the continued abundance of other species in the same habitat.

Sooty Dancer *(Argia lugens)*

FAMILY: Coenagrionidae (Pond Damsels)
LENGTH: 1½–2 inches
FLIGHT SEASON: Apr. 8–Nov. 10
DISTRIBUTION: throughout the region (apparently not yet recorded in NV but should occur there)

Female

"What's the big, black damselfly on that boulder?" This question points out three clues for identifying a male Sooty Dancer, one of our most easily recognized damselflies. The word *lugens* is Latin for "mourning," and a number of other black animals have this word in their scientific names. They are large and, as their scien-

Male

tific name suggests, adult males are nearly all black, except for narrow, pale rings where the middle abdominal segments meet. Young males and females may be light brown or pale blue, with black or dark red markings. On all but the darkest males, note the shoulder stripe; as with Dusky Dancer (see page 56), the stripe is split throughout its length. However, on Sooty Dancer, the two branches are of similar thickness, and many individuals have a crossbar that turns the parallel stripes into an "H."

A southwestern species, Sooty Dancers have a broad elevational range and may be encountered from sea level to about 6,000 feet. They usually occupy sunny cobble- or boulder-strewn waters, from small streams to large rivers. Occasionally, they occur near streams in deep woods, or away from water on rocky hillsides or even parking lots.

Fiery-eyed Dancer *(Argia oenea)*
FAMILY: Coenagrionidae (Pond Damsels)
LENGTH: 1¼–1½ inches
FLIGHT SEASON: May 17–Nov. 16
DISTRIBUTION: TX, NM, AZ, CH, SO

Its cherry-red eyes make the bluish-purple and black Fiery-eyed Dancer the easiest of the region's dancers to identify. Only one other U.S. dancer has similar eyes, and it occurs in central Texas. This colorful species' scientific name is derived from the Greek word *oinos* (wine), referring to the metallic red color of the male's thorax. Small, clear streams at several thousand feet elevation are its favorite haunts. This species occurs in the drier parts of Arizona, in a diagonal band from the southeastern to the northwestern part of the state. Additionally, there is a small, newly discovered population in the Big Bend region of west Texas. Watch for territorial males guarding a stretch of water from a boulder in a stream channel. Group egg-laying is common; often, a dozen or more tandem pairs will crowd onto a patch of watercress leaves as the females deposit their eggs.

Springwater Dancer *(Argia plana)*
FAMILY: Coenagrionidae (Pond Damsels)
LENGTH: 1¼–1⅜ inches
FLIGHT SEASON: Mar. 18–Nov. 20
DISTRIBUTION: TX, NM, AZ, CO, SO, CH

Vivid Dancer *(Argia vivida)*
FAMILY: Coenagrionidae (Pond Damsels)
LENGTH: 1⅛–1½ inches
FLIGHT SEASON: Jan. 2–Nov. 15
DISTRIBUTION: NM, CO, UT, NV, AZ, CA, BN

On mountain streams of the Southwest, the Springwater Dancer may be the most numerous damselfly. This adaptable species is found in various habitats from Wisconsin to Guatemala. Depending on the temperature, males show various hues of purple. Most individuals have an unforked shoulder

stripe. The abdomen has black rings, small black dashes on the sides of the central segments, and a purple tip. The more heavily built females (shown here) often have a blue tip to the abdomen. Farther east, males of this species are a bright sky-blue, one of just a few damsels to show such geographic variation. Once thought to occur throughout the western U.S., it is now known that the westernmost representatives represent another species, the Vivid Dancer (*Argia vivida*). It occurs westward from New Mexico, Colorado, and Nebraska to the Pacific Ocean, south into Baja California Norte, and north into southwestern Canada. Females of both species may be blue or brown. In the few areas where both species might occur together (locally in Colorado, New Mexico, or northern Arizona) they should be distinguished by examining the male's terminal appendages; on Vivid, the downward-projecting portion of the upper appendage is tapered and pointed, as opposed to shorter and more rounded with a small tooth on Springwater.

Sabino Dancer *(Argia sabino)*
FAMILY: Coenagrionidae (Pond Damsels)
LENGTH: 1⅜–1⅝ inches
FLIGHT SEASON: May 16–Oct. 4
DISTRIBUTION: AZ, SO

The Sabino Dancer is a rare southwestern odonate. It flies in Sonora and in the lower mountains of southeastern Arizona at elevations where plants such as saguaro cacti and ocotillos mix with oaks and junipers. Both sexes have a Y-shaped shoulder stripe that's deeply forked at the upper end. An unusual characteristic for any dancer: individuals from the same populations may have the "Y" intact, or the lower arm of the fork may be broken like the losing side of a wishbone. Segment seven of the abdomen is black, and eight through ten are blue; nonetheless, Sabino Dancer resembles several other species, including Tarascan Dancer (*A. tarascana*, not treated here and also very rare in the U.S.); thus, the shape and spacing of its terminal appendages should be examined through a hand lens to confirm identification.

Named for its discovery site at Sabino Canyon in northeastern Tucson, this damselfly was described to science in 1994. Both males and females perch prominently on boulders at streamside and roadside. Nonetheless, scientists who searched for it in the canyon found it to be extremely rare and occasionally absent, suggesting that its populations may be especially sensitive to rainfall and water levels. This species is usually found in streams where waterfalls have carved plunge-basin pools into the underlying rock. At such pools, it may persist for a while after the stream has stopped flowing. After its discovery, forest fires in 2002 and 2003 burned over 85,000 mountainous acres above Sabino Canyon. Subsequent flooding and runoff in 2003 and 2005 blanketed the canyon bottom with ash, mud, and charred debris that may forever change the character of the stream. Fortunately, this species is now known from several more sites in Arizona and Sonora.

Blue-ringed Dancer *(Argia sedula)*

Female

FAMILY: Coenagrionidae (Pond Damsels)
LENGTH: 1⅛–1⅜ inches
FLIGHT SEASON: Feb. 10–Dec. 2
DISTRIBUTION: throughout the region

A characteristic damsel of flowing water is the Blue-ringed Dancer, its name referring to the pale blue ring at the junction of each abdominal segment. This successful species is found from the northeastern U.S. to southern California on both tiny streams and large rivers, appearing only occasionally at ponds. Blue-ringed Dancer is often abundant on trails or open areas near the water, especially early in the morning. Its abdomen

Male

has a pale blue tip and a similarly colored dash on most segments. The eyes and the black-banded thorax are deep blue, and the wings may have a pale yellow tint.

Dusky Dancer *(Argia translata)*

FAMILY: Coenagrionidae (Pond Damsels)
LENGTH: 1¼–1½ inches
FLIGHT SEASON: May 1–Nov. 18
DISTRIBUTION: TX, NM, AZ, CH, SO

Perhaps the most widespread odonate in the Western Hemisphere, Dusky Dancer occurs from the Maritime Provinces of Canada to Argentina. Widespread in the eastern U.S., it becomes local in the Southwest but may be abundant. As common as it may be in Arizona and Sonora, it should also be watched for in southern California and northern Baja California.

Adult male Dusky Dancers are one of our few black damselflies, with only narrow, pale blue rings where the abdominal segments meet, and deep-purple eyes. They are most similar to the extremely local and black-eyed Tezpi Dancer (*A. tezpi,* not discussed here) and the much larger Sooty Dancer (see page 53). Young males and females are light brown or brown with some blue markings; old males may develop a pale overlay of pruinescence. Females exhibit useful identification marks at both ends. The shoulder stripe on the thorax is split into two parallel stripes—the lower is usually thicker—that join just above the legs. Also, the pale tip of the abdomen has a black lateral band on segments eight, nine, and ten. Although usually associated with streams or river margins, and occasionally found at lake edges, females and immatures are often seen perched at branch tips along wooded trails some distance from water, and this habit is a useful identification clue as well. Mats of watercress on small streams are a favored egg-laying site, and dozens of pairs may be seen ovipositing together. Note that tandem males guarding their mates become paler, revealing a female-like striped thoracic pattern. This is the opposite of what is observed in some other dancers (Blue-ringed Dancer, for example) where tandem males become much darker, obscuring their thoracic stripes. Because darkened males are less visible to predators during mating, it is not clear why male Dusky Dancers turn pale.

Double-striped Bluet
(*Enallagma basidens*)

FAMILY: Coenagrionidae (Pond Damsels)
LENGTH: ¾–1 inch
FLIGHT SEASON: Mar. 28–Nov. 20
DISTRIBUTION: TX, NM, AZ, CA, CO,
  NV, CH

The tiny Double-striped Bluet is the smallest North American member of its genus and one of our smallest damselflies. When perched alongside any other bluet, its minute stature is obvious. It is found most often at grassy pond or lake edges, where it may be very common. Other places to look for it include quiet backwaters of rivers and the vegetated margins of canals. This species occurs from sea level up to at least 3,000 feet, occasionally at mineralized water. During windy conditions, it often takes shelter in shrubbery near water. Once closely seen, it is readily identified; besides being tiny, on both sexes the usual black shoulder stripe is divided in two by a thin blue or tan crack-like stripe. The bright blue eyespots behind the compound eyes are connected by a bar of the same color. Texas may have been the original stronghold of this species in the U.S. However, during the twentieth century, it spread dramatically, now occurring eastward to Florida and New York, westward to extreme southern California, and north to the province of Ontario. Its increase may have been aided by the many ponds, lakes, and canals that have been added to the landscape, but this expansion has not been noted in many other damselflies. This species has not yet been recorded in Sonora (Mexico) but it probably occurs there.

Tule Bluet *(Enallagma carunculatum)*

FAMILY: Coenagrionidae (Pond Damsels)
LENGTH: 1–1½ inches
FLIGHT SEASON: Feb. 19–Dec. 26
DISTRIBUTION: most of the region; not
    yet known from far west TX, CH, or SO

Tule Bluet is found throughout much of the Southwest and across the northern U.S. It inhabits lake edges—where it may be abundant; less frequently it is found at ponds or river margins. This species often occurs with other very similar bluets, and a hand lens will aid greatly with identification. Tule Bluet is darker overall than Familiar Bluet (see next entry) and has different terminal appendages. Unlike the uniformly patterned Arroyo Bluet (see page 59), the frontmost several black rings on the abdomen are usually separated by wider blue areas, and this irregularity makes it appear a bit lighter overall. As with most female bluets, the black marks on the dorsal surface of the abdomen are much more extensive. Without microscopic examination of the mesostigmal plates, most female bluets are likely to go unidentified. The male's upper terminal appendages are blunt, appearing like small, pale pillows.

Familiar Bluet *(Enallagma civile)*

FAMILY: Coenagrionidae (Pond Damsels)
LENGTH: 1⅛–1¼
FLIGHT SEASON: throughout the year
DISTRIBUTION: throughout the region

Female

The bluets are our most frequently seen damselflies, especially Familiar Bluet, one of the largest Southwest bluets. Dozens to thousands can be seen at lake edges, where they hang onto swaying grasses like tiny flags. Because of its narrow, black abdominal rings, Familiar Bluet appears very bright

Male

blue, even at a distance. Other species such as Arroyo (see next entry), Tule (see previous entry), and the very small Double-striped Bluet (see page 57) have black rings that are wider, or elongated forward as tiny arrows—making them appear darker from above. Additionally, the male Familiar's large upper terminal abdominal appendages (cerci) appear fan-like rather than as narrow hooks or spines, and these may be seen in binoculars.

Arroyo Bluet *(Enallagma praevarum)*
FAMILY: Coenagrionidae (Pond Damsels)
LENGTH: 1–1⅜ inches
FLIGHT SEASON: Feb. 20–Nov. 25
DISTRIBUTION: throughout the region

The Arroyo Bluet is a common southwestern species found throughout the region and eastward to central Texas. Unlike the bright-blue Familiar Bluet (see previous entry) with which it is often found, this species is smaller, a bit more slender, and with broader black markings above, making it appear darker in the field. The blue and black abdominal bands are evenly spaced, unlike the pattern of Tule Bluet (see page 58). The Arroyo Bluet's eyespots are variable and may be separated or connected by a bar. Through a hand lens, note in side view that the cerci of Arroyo Bluet are forked; those of Familiar Bluet are rather broad and fan-like. Arroyo Bluet may be very common in its preferred open and arid habitats but is often outnumbered by Familiar Bluet. Watch for it from sea level to at least 5,000 feet elevation in a variety of wetlands, including vegetated backwaters of larger rivers, small streams, ornamental water features, and vegetated pond edges—even those polluted by livestock.

Painted Damsel
(Hesperagrion heterodoxum)
FAMILY: Coenagrionidae (Pond Damsels)
LENGTH: 1–1⅜ inches
FLIGHT SEASON: Mar. 8–Nov. 30
DISTRIBUTION: TX, NM, CO, AZ, CH, SO

Adorned in black, red, and bright blue, the gaudy Painted Damsel is the most striking of the Southwest damselflies. This miniature beauty is one of the best arguments in favor of buying a pair of close-focus binoculars. Its immatures are also attractive, at first the color of orange sherbet, but then quickly developing the adults' coloration. Females are similar to males but lack their red tones and could be confused with one of the female forktails. Painted Damsels breed in a variety of habitats and at various elevations from sunny desert creeks to sycamore-shaded mountain streams. They're usually found in the grasses or sedges bordering springs and the slower backwaters of larger rivers, but may turn up in the sparse vegetation growing around an overflowing windmill, or at a back-yard pond.

Desert Forktail *(Ischnura barberi)*

FAMILY: Coenagrionidae (Pond Damsels)

LENGTH: 1–1½ inches

FLIGHT SEASON: Mar. 4–Nov. 19

DISTRIBUTION: probably throughout the region; not yet recorded in CH but occurs nearby in El Paso, TX

Female

Known mainly from the U.S. Southwest and several sites in northern Sonora, the Desert Forktail is only infrequently encountered and not well known. At freshwater habitats it is outnumbered by other damselflies, including the very similar and more widespread Rambur's Forktail (see next entry). Elsewhere, its success may lie with its ability to survive at salty or mineralized locations that are unattractive to

Male

other damsels. This colorful species inhabits arid habitats from sea level (or below at the Salton Sea) to high desert or plateau elevations of several thousand feet. Look for it at desert springs—especially mineralized ones—and associated pools, green and perhaps stagnant ponds at water-treatment plants, salty lakes such as those at or near the Salton Sea in southern California, and marine habitats such as mudflat margins along the Gulf of California or the coast of southernmost California. Males are colorful; the eyes alone are black above, rich blue centrally, and pale green below. The thorax has a black mid-dorsal stripe margined by pale green, and then black shoulder stripes. The entire lower portion of the thorax, the first two abdominal segments, and segments eight and nine are very pale blue or blue-green. The rest of the abdomen is pale orange with narrow black dorsal stripes—each constricted toward the rear—allowing even more orange to show. Young females are tan or pale red, later resembling the males or becoming pale brown with black stripes on the abdomen. Most likely to be confused with the darker Rambur's Forktail; in hand, note the terminal abdominal segments. On male Desert Forktails the paraprocts (the lower pair) appear as short spines that curve upward; on Rambur's they are straight.

Rambur's Forktail *(Ischnura ramburii)*

FAMILY: Coenagrionidae (Pond Damsels)
LENGTH: 1–1½ inches
FLIGHT SEASON: Mar. 9–Dec. 8
DISTRIBUTION: TX, NM, AZ, CA, CH;
  not yet recorded in SO or BN

Occurring from New England well into South America, this species' U.S. stronghold is along the Eastern Seaboard and in the Southeast. In the Southwest, Rambur's Forktail is decidedly local, where it inhabits stream, irrigation canal, pond, and lake edges and slower stretches of large rivers. When encountered, it may be the most common damselfly present. In southern California, it is primarily a desert species. Look for it from near sea level to several thousand feet elevation.

Adult male Rambur's Forktails have a green-and-black-striped thorax much like that of Desert Forktail, but Rambur's black stripes are broader. The abdomen appears darker from above on Rambur's, because it lacks the Desert Forktail's constricted dorsal stripes. Eastern populations of Rambur's often exhibit black above on segment nine; western individuals usually show blue. Female Rambur's occur in three color forms, one of which changes dramatically with age. Many young females are orange to tomato-red, with a black stripe atop the abdomen. These mature into dull-colored adults that are largely pale olive-green, tan, and black. The third form resembles a colorful mature male, but note the broader abdomen and its thicker tip.

Citrine Forktail *(Ischnura hastata)*

FAMILY: Coenagrionidae (Pond Damsels)
LENGTH: ¾–1 inch
FLIGHT SEASON: Jan. 10–Nov. 20
DISTRIBUTION: TX, NM, CO, AZ, CA,
  CH, SO, BN

Female

The only southwestern forktail with a yellow abdomen, the diminutive Citrine Forktail is the region's smallest damselfly. Common in the eastern U.S. and south to northern South America, this diminutive species has reached such far-flung islands as the Galapagos, Bermuda, and the Azores.

Male

Locally, it ranges westward through southern California—usually close to the Mexican border—and is sparse in northwest Mexico. Not much longer than an eyelash, it takes a practiced eye to find this colorful species. Although most commonly seen at grassy pond edges, windy weather may scatter them through brushy fields. The young females are orange with black on the top of the thorax and near the end of the abdomen; at this stage they resemble several other species, but their small size, limited black, and the company they keep aid with their identification.

Female Pacific Forktail

Pacific Forktail *(Ischnura cervula)*
FAMILY: Coenagrionidae (Pond Damsels)
LENGTH: 1–1¼ inches
FLIGHT SEASON: throughout the year
DISTRIBUTION: NM, AZ, CO, UT, NV, CA, SO, BN

Male Pacific Forktail

Plains Forktail *(Ischnura damula)*
FAMILY: Coenagrionidae (Pond Damsels)
LENGTH: ⅞–1⅜ inches
FLIGHT SEASON: Feb. 9–Oct. 29
DISTRIBUTION: TX, NM, CO, UT, AZ, CH, SO

Pacific Forktail and Plains Forktail are look-alike species that occur in much of the Southwest. Both inhabit the western Great Plains to the eastern slope of the Rocky Mountains; additionally, Pacific Forktail is widespread in the westernmost states. Males of each species sport a sky-blue thorax that's glossy black above. The black is broken by four tiny blue dots that form the corners of a square. Females are variable; the black-striped thorax may be pale blue or pink, or the female may resemble the male. Both inhabit grassy or weedy pond or lake edges, streams and flowing irrigation channels, and the weedy backwaters of larger rivers. Additionally, either species may occur, often in numbers, in brushy habitat near lake edges. To identify them in hand, note the cerci in side view; those of Plains Forktail are rather large and fan-shaped, looking a bit like a boot with the toe pointing downward. Those of Pacific are small, with a slender thumb-like projection that points downward.

Western Forktail *(Ischnura perparva)*
FAMILY: Coenagrionidae (Pond Damsels)
LENGTH: ⅞–1¼ inches
FLIGHT SEASON: Mar. 2–Nov. 6
DISTRIBUTION: NM, AZ, CO, UT, NV,
   CA, recently in BN

Mexican Forktail *(Ischnura demorsa)*
FAMILY: Coenagrionidae (Pond Damsels)
LENGTH: ⅞–1 inch
FLIGHT SEASON: Feb. 10–Dec. 2
DISTRIBUTION: TX, NM, CO, UT, NV,
   AZ, CH, SO

Two small and very similar forktails are
found in the Southwest. Both inhabit fresh-
water and mineralized ponds, stream edges, springs, seeps below dams, quieter backwaters of rivers, and marshy areas. The Western Forktail is a widespread western
species; however, it is rare along the border, except in extreme southwestern California.
This species has a great elevational range, occurring from sea level to at least 8,000
feet. The very similar Mexican Forktail is a true Southwest species, occurring most
often in more arid habitats from western Oklahoma and Nebraska into Arizona. It
inhabits upland deserts and plains, scrubby foothills, and mountain forests of oaks or
conifers. In the U.S., it is more likely to be seen from perhaps 1,500 to at least 6,000
feet, but it has been taken in the state of Sonora at only 80 feet above sea level. Males
of both species have a mint-green to blue-green thorax with black dorsal and shoulder
stripes. From above, most of the abdomen is black, with pale rings where the segments
join. Segments eight and nine are bright blue and ten is black above and blue below.
Both species have a black line on the side of segment eight and a line or spot on the
side of segment nine. The Western Forktail is likely to be more heavily marked on segment nine. To be certain of identification, check the terminal appendages. In side
view, the paraprocts of the Western are short (not extending past the downcurved
cerci) and uniformly forked. In the Mexican Forktail, the upper arm of the fork is very
long and extends well beyond the cerci. Females are difficult to identify and may
resemble males; they may be orange with black markings, or deep pruinose blue.

Desert Firetail *(Telebasis salva)*
FAMILY: Coenagrionidae (Pond Damsels)
LENGTH: ⅞–1⅛ inches

FLIGHT SEASON: Mar. 19–Dec. 18
DISTRIBUTION: throughout the region

The genus *Telebasis* is a large group of tropical damselflies that are largely red. In the U.S., one is widespread in the West. Although its name suggests a desert dweller, the Desert Firetail may be found along shady mountain streams or at pools sur-

Female

rounded by lush woodlands. In the Southwest, this species is often numerous at pond edges (including overgrazed livestock ponds), weedy or grassy stretches of slow-moving water, marshes, and even back-yard lily ponds. You aren't likely to misidentify the small, slender, cherry-red males (females are tan but are usually found among the males). The Western Red Damsel (*Amphia-*

Male

grion abbreviatum, not featured in this book), which is only spottily distributed in the Southwest, is somewhat similar but has a thick, stubby body, and is hairy and black on top of its thorax. Immature Painted Damsel (see page 59) and immature Black-and-white Damsel (see page 53) are orange, not red. The latter has a more elongate body and a striped thorax.

SHADOWDAMSELS (FAMILY PLATYSTICTIDAE)

The Shadowdamsels are members of a large tropical family found in both the Eastern and Western Hemispheres. Males are long and slender, with an abdomen that may be more than twice the wing length. Females, as in most damsels, are thicker-bodied. Most are inconspicuous—the U.S. name for the family refers to some species' habit of taking shelter in shaded sites. In other countries, they have been referred to as "forest damsels."

Desert Shadowdamsel
(Palaemnema domina)
FAMILY: Platystictidae (Shadowdamsels)
LENGTH: 1⅜–1¾ inches
FLIGHT SEASON: July 17–Sept. 21
DISTRIBUTION: AZ, SO

One of the real specialties of the desert Southwest is the Desert Shadowdamsel. Forty or so members of its family—all in the genus *Palaemnema*—are found in the Americas; only this one has reached the U.S. Here it is known from several streams in southeast Arizona and a few additional sites in northwest Mexico. Both sexes have a bright blue abdomen patterned with black; the male is longer-bodied. Although most Odonata are active in sunny habitats, some shadowdamsels fly in subdued light—and occasionally even during light rain showers. Indeed, most U.S. sightings of this species have been during the late-summer monsoon season, a time of the year characterized by afternoon thunderstorms. During much of the time, these damsels remain in deep shade, such as the root masses of trees that have fallen at the water's edge. This species has clear wings; however, some other members of the family have wings patterned with black.

THREADTAILS (FAMILY PROTONEURIDAE)

The threadtails, known in other countries as pinflies, are members of a family of about 350 species that occur throughout the tropics. Often colorful, they are not easily seen, partly because many have an extremely slender abdomen and partly because of their behavior, hanging in the shadows from branch tips or patrolling rapidly over sun-dappled water where they are almost impossible to follow with the eye. Perched individuals may be seen in foliage, but only with practice and some degree of luck. Threadtails hover, an uncommon behavior among our damselflies. If you can find a male lingering motionless over the water, aim your binoculars at it as quickly as possible and you may be rewarded with a long, satisfying view. Most conspicuous are the tandem pairs laying eggs on bits of floating bark or aquatic plants. Note that the female's long abdomen is usually bent at an impossibly sharp angle, looking as if it's about to break in half. A tandem male is often attached to her by nothing more than his claspers—his rigid body angled forward.

Three threadtails range northward into the southern U.S., barely reaching the region in west Texas. Two of these are also found in Sonora—one very close to the border.

Orange-striped Threadtail
(*Protoneura cara*)
FAMILY: Protoneuridae (Threadtails)
LENGTH: 1¼–1½ inches
FLIGHT SEASON: late Apr.–Oct.
DISTRIBUTION: TX, SO; not yet recorded
    in CH

The Orange-striped Threadtail has been found in the Río Yaqui drainage of Sonora, less than seventy-five miles south of the Arizona border. During a very wet year, this northernmost population could follow the river to its headwaters and appear in southeastern Arizona or southwestern New Mexico. This fine species demands close inspection. Males have red eyes, an orange-and-black-striped thorax, orange legs, and a long, glossy black abdomen ringed with orange. The females resemble the males but have a thicker abdomen and are not as brightly colored. Like many threadtails, it flies at the margins of large rivers, as well as along tiny streams. Watch for it where currents deposit plant debris along the bank, as this is an ideal egg-laying site.

Dragonflies captured the imagination of the peoples of the Southwest and elsewhere long before the appearance of modern science. Stylized dragonflies—a vertical line crossed by one or two horizontal lines—appeared frequently in rock art created by the earliest Americans. In some cases, the exact meaning of these symbols is unknown but may be inferred from the writings of early explorers or the modern-day interpretations of tribal beliefs. In other cases, the exact meanings will never be revealed. For example, there are well-executed dragonfly images on bowls placed in burial sites of the Mogollon Mimbres, a tribe most numerous in southwest New Mexico. But the Mimbres disappeared during the mid-1100s (long before European explorers began to document the Southwest peoples) and left no clues as to the meaning of their art. It is known that many of the Mimbres pueblos and smaller homesites were built near permanent water—for which the dragonfly may have been emblematic. Or, because dragonflies were often associated with the spirit world, perhaps they were left with the dead as guides to the other side.

More recent tribes such as the Cheyenne people of the Great Plains (who ranged as far south as southern Colorado) adorned their clothing, shields, horses, and bodies with dragonfly images in order to share or evoke their powers. For example, a pair of moccasins worn into battle might be decorated with dragonflies, conferring the wearer with speed and agility. The Cheyenne regarded these insects as fast and difficult to capture or kill, and their darting flight suggested the ability to avoid bullets. Thus, dragonfly paintings or amulets could grant the bearer protection from enemies.

The dragonfly's intimate relationship with water did not go unnoticed. The Hopis associated them with springs, and the Navajos often depicted them around a pool of water. Cheyenne dancers were painted with dragonflies, which, along with various background colors, represented clouds, wind, and life-giving water. Additionally, the Cheyennes took note of dragonflies hunting in circling swarms over water and made them a symbol of the whirlwind—which could provide information such as the direction in which to travel. The tribes of the Northern Plains considered it good luck when a dragonfly landed on a tipi, as that signified a nearby source of water.

Their dexterous flight and seemingly frenetic activity earned dragonflies a reputation for skill, swiftness, and restlessness. An often-cited Zuni myth, in which a toy dragonfly comes to life, depicts dragonflies as messengers between humans and the gods. This relationship between dragonflies and the spirit or dream world appears widespread among the native peoples of the American West. Like butterflies, dragonflies have been associated with regeneration, transformation, birth, and death—traits suggested by their emergence from the water and their annual cycle of appearance and disappearance.

Indeed, odonates do seem well adapted to transcend many threats to their survival. Despite the tremendous demands on the Southwest's water, dragonflies continue to flourish and, where water is provided to formerly dry areas, certain species may actually expand their ranges. For example: the Roseate Skimmer, a pink-and-purple dragonfly once found only in the southeastern U.S., has traveled northward from Mexico and now ranges into southern California and Baja California Norte. Its spread was aided perhaps by the thousands of livestock ponds, roadside ditches, water-treatment plants, and irrigated fields that now dot the area. Such range extensions may have been going on longer than we'd suspect: earlier inhabitants of the Southwest created irrigation systems as long as 3,000 years ago, and the ranges of various dragonflies may have begun to change back then. Even now, the ranges of various Odonata continue to expand and contract. Especially where rainfall is unpredictable, dragonfly populations may appear and disappear; ponds and streams may appear and disappear; they may dry out for years at a time, only to be quickly repopulated after heavy rains.

Dragonflies are recognized by nearly everyone, and their distinctive form has become one of the most familiar icons of the natural world. Everywhere you look, their shimmering wings, bulbous eyes, and pastel-hued bodies embellish stylish dresses, notecards, garden ornaments, ceramics, and stained glass. Jewelers create them with all manner of gems and precious metals, and countless others are inked into tender skin. At the water's edge their beauty, speed, and acrobatic flight entertain hikers and anglers, while their metamorphoses and brief adult lives inspire poets. Deeply embedded in the mythology and symbolism of the Southwest, they were revered as messengers to the spirit world.

The best way to really appreciate dragonflies is to spend some time watching them. Seven- or eight-power close-focus binoculars will provide astonishing views from a distance at which most dragonflies continue to behave naturally. (See "Useful Websites," page 77, for sites with tips on choosing binoculars.) However, if you move slowly, many species may be approached closely—sometimes to within several inches.

In the temperate regions of the world, dragonflies appear with the first sunny days of spring, becoming most numerous during the long and sultry days of summer. In the northernmost or southernmost latitudes, a dragonfly's entire flight season may be limited to just a few weeks each year. Along the U.S.–Mexico border, we are fortunate because dragonflies and damselflies are on the wing during most of the year—although in colder areas they may be absent from about October to March or April.

Television Westerns portray the Southwest as a realm of parched deserts punctuated by the occasional cactus or bleached cow skull—not exactly a haven for aquatic insects. In reality, the region offers a varied mosaic of landforms, nearly all of which have some kind of wetlands associated with them. Habitats for dragonflies include: both concrete- and cottonwood-lined rivers, reservoirs created for recreation or to generate power, spring-fed marshes or *cienegas*, shallow mineral-rich evaporation basins, irrigation canals, temporarily wet desert washes, water-treatment facilities, natural lakes, mountain streams shaded by immense sycamores, livestock and golf course ponds, and ornamental water features ranging from industrial-park reflecting pools to tiny back-yard lily ponds.

By definition, dragonflies are cold-blooded and cannot fly until the air around them warms their bodies. Therefore, they are usually inactive during the cool, early mornings, hiding in inconspicuous nighttime perches, disappearing among grasses or leafy branches. An exception to the rule, some of the larger species such as darners can warm themselves with heat generated by their flight muscles; these may be the first species you see flying in the morning. As the sun rises and the air warms (65–70 degrees F should do it), dragonflies and damselflies become energized and their daily activities begin.

Most individuals you'll see at the water's edge are territorial males. Territories may be anything from a few square feet of grasses (many damselflies) to several hundred feet of roadside or river edge (spiketails, river cruisers), and are often uniformly spaced. Most dragonflies remain within their own territories. Some species are non-territorial, never returning to the same perch. Occasionally, you'll find large aggregations of odonates. During a windy day you may see dozens of dragonflies clinging to the sheltered side of a shrub, or thousands of bluets that have been blown across a pond and are densely stacked up on waterside vegetation.

Like many birds, certain dragonflies hunt from and return to a well-situated branch, weed tip, or an open spot on the ground. Examples of such perchers include the king skimmers, amberwings, and setwings, which may return repeatedly to a favored perch. These may include artificial structures; members of the clubtail and skimmer families often perch on fences, telephone wires, and even car antennae. Less likely to perch, certain darners, emeralds, and skimmers such as the saddlebags and rainpool gliders spend most of the day in the air, touching down only infrequently; these have been characterized as fliers, as opposed to perchers. If the day becomes very sunny, you'll see many dragonflies of the perching type assume the obelisk position, pointing their abdomens skyward. Obelisking reduces the amount of solar energy striking the body—one way a dragonfly keeps from overheating. Damselflies, on the other hand, are not likely to obelisk.

If you approach slowly and avoid throwing a warning shadow, you may find yourself at arm's length from your quarry. Note that rather than sitting motionless, dragonflies frequently move their heads, watching for both predators and prey. Females of many odonates are less frequently seen, usually approaching the water when they are ready to mate. Look for them in nearby weedy growth—where they may be joined by immature males not yet ready to defend a territory at the water's edge. Early in the morning or during windy weather, spend some time walking through vegetation near the water. You may find large numbers of both dragonflies and damselflies taking shelter in tall grasses or stands of rank plants such as ragweed, sunflower, or goldenrod.

Notice that while hunting or searching for mates, dragonflies can hover, fly backwards, make astonishingly sharp turns, and accelerate from a standstill to over twenty miles per hour in the blink of an eye. The Odonata owe their spectacular flight prowess to one of their most primitive characteristics—the complex musculature that controls their wings. These muscles, anchored to the floor of the thorax, allow all four wings to move independently, providing the Odonata with their extraordinary maneuverability.

As you watch odonates, occasionally you will see a male curl the tip of his abdomen downward then forward to his second abdominal segment. As he does this, he transfers sperm to where his penis is located. When a receptive female comes to the water to lay her eggs, one or more potential mates will quickly approach her, often precipitating spectacular territorial battles. Before long, a male will snatch the female from the air and grasp her with the appendages at the end of his abdomen. If she is receptive, she will attach the tip of her abdomen to his second abdominal segment and receive his sperm. Some Odonata mate in the air; others hang from vegetation. The characteristic mating posture is known as the "wheel" position. Mating damselflies, especially, have a heart-shaped mating posture, and in Asia, this has been referred to as the "heart" position. Mating may last an hour or more—or be over in a matter of seconds. It is a very lucky photographer, indeed, who has photos of mating king skimmers, dragonflies whose copulation in flight is over in the blink of an eye. During prolonged mating, male

Black Meadowhawks (a widespread species that enters the northern portion of the Southwest) copulating

Odonata spend time scraping away sperm from previous copulations in order to replace it with their own. Once mating is over, the female releases the tip of her abdomen from his body. Often, they will remain in tandem and he will continue to guard her from nearby males.

Mating is followed by the laying of several batches of eggs. In many families of Odonata, the male guards the female as she lays her eggs. Darners and various damselflies will alight on vegetation to lay their eggs, making the adults targets for predators. Spiketails lay their eggs in the sediment of streams, hidden, for the time being, from hungry fishes. Other dragonflies will touch the water briefly, depositing an egg here or there—their rapid flight protecting them from some predators.

Odonata don't live forever. Eventually, repeated mating and aerial battles take their toll. Wings become tattered, fat reserves are depleted, and dragonflies become less adept at escaping danger.

Ovipositing Dusky Dancers

WATER GARDENS AS DRAGONFLY PONDS

Although traveling to various wetlands can be an exciting aspect of dragonfly watching, so is the satisfaction of creating a habitat that attracts dragonflies to you. Artificial wetlands developed by homeowners include lily ponds, water gardens, and water features. They can be anything from a large metal tub with a few sprigs of greenery to an elaborately landscaped lake with islands, bridges, and all manner of aquatic plants. In any case, as long as the weather is warm and sunny, dragonflies will appear, providing the aquatic gardener with hours of entertainment. As a bonus, your habitat will become a home for other interesting insects such as water striders and various aquatic beetles, and your plantings may attract butterflies. If your pond is large enough, don't be surprised to hear frogs or toads singing there on a warm summer evening.

Livestock watering tanks or troughs, half whisky barrels (now available with plastic liners), and a variety of fountains may be placed aboveground—alleviating the need for digging a hole. Pre-formed pond shells that hold several hundred gallons of water are available in a variety of shapes. These may be purchased at hardware or pond-supply stores and may be buried to their upper lip or kept aboveground. Larger ponds are usually made with a sheet of rubber liner that's set into an excavation. This type of construction provides the most options for size, depth, and shape. Do-it-yourselfers who don't live on very hard or rocky ground may enjoy digging their own ponds, but larger projects often require the participation of a landscape specialist with a backhoe.

Most people enjoy hearing a spray of water or a small waterfall, both of which will attract songbirds and hummingbirds to bathe. This can be accomplished with a small pump that may also circulate the pond's water through a filter. Running water will also discourage mosquitoes, whose larvae breathe at the surface of calm water. Lacking moving water, the same may be accomplished by stocking the pond with a few mosquitofish (Gambusia), live-bearing cousins of guppies. The addition of products such as Mosquito Dunks will discourage mosquitoes but are harmless to dragonflies and other wildlife. Larger fishes such as bass, bluegill, and koi should be avoided whenever possible as they will disturb or eat your plants, dine on your dragonfly larvae, and even snap up any adult dragonflies or damselflies that come to the surface while laying eggs.

Useful Websites
www.fishpondinfo.com/pond.htm
http://bigsnestpond.net
www.angelfrogs.com
www.dragonflysoc.org.uk/frameset.htm?mhd1&home

DRAGONFLY WATCHING: NATURE FESTIVALS, ORGANIZATIONS, AND PLACES TO VISIT

• • • • • •

The following organizations and events (including several in south Texas) provide dragonfly-related experiences lasting several hours to several days. All are geared toward amateurs.

Boyce Thompson Arboretum, Superior, Arizona Several naturalist-led dragonfly walks are offered during summer. The arboretum grounds provide good dragonfly habitat. http://arboretum.ag.arizona.edu

Southern California Field trips, classes, and wildlife-pond tours are posted occasionally at Kathy Biggs's website. www.sonic.net/~bigsnest/Pond/dragons/PROGRAM.html

Dragonfly Days, Weslaco, Texas A May weekend of dragonfly presentations and field trips in south Texas. www.valleynaturecenter.org

Dragonfly Festival, Bitter Lake National Wildlife Refuge, Roswell, New Mexico Held in late August, this event offers two days of dragonfly, bird, and other natural-history events. www.rt66.com/~kjherman/fbl/df.html

NatureQuest, Concan, Texas Held during late April in the Texas Hill Country, this weeklong nature festival usually offers a dragonfly talk and two dragonfly field trips. Check the website for additional fall events as well. www.thcrr.com

Southeastern Arizona Butterfly Association (SEABA) Several field trips offer dragonfly opportunities or a combination of dragonfly and butterfly viewing. www.naba.org/chapters/nabasa/home.html

Southwest Wings Birding Festival, Sierra Vista, Arizona Held during early August, this nature festival usually includes a dragonfly presentation and one or two dragonfly or dragonfly-butterfly field trips. www.swwings.org

Texas Butterfly Festival, Mission, Texas Held during mid to late October since the mid 1990s, it usually includes a dragonfly presentation and two to four dragonfly field trips. Pre- or post-festival butterfly tours may offer additional dragonfly-viewing opportunities in northeast Mexico. www.texasbutterfly.com

Verde Valley Birding and Nature Festival, Cottonwood, Arizona A four-day event held during late April. Recently, dragonfly-butterfly walks have been offered, and other festival events visit productive dragonfly habitats. www.birdyverde.org

World Birding Center: Bentsen-Rio Grande Valley State Park, Mission, Texas Dragonfly walks may be available on a weekly basis or more often, depending on staff availability. Visitors will find good dragonfly habitat on the grounds as well as at other nearby sites. www.worldbirdingcenter.org/sites/mission

Yuma Birding and Nature Festival, Yuma, Arizona This southwest Arizona festival is held during mid to late April. A three-day nature event, it includes a dragonfly seminar and field trip. www.yumabirding.org

The Dragonfly Society of the Americas (D.S.A.) Information concerning national and regional meetings, including field trips, is published in *Argia*, the society's quarterly newsletter. www.odonatacentral.org

GLOSSARY

• • • • • •

Abdomen The posteriormost main region of the body, composed of ten segments (sometimes referred to by number) and the terminal appendages.

Anisoptera The suborder of the Odonata that contains the dragonflies.

Bars Markings that cross the body from side to side.

Border Southwest The geographic area covered in the text: west Texas east to the Big Bend region, New Mexico, Arizona, southern California, and in Mexico, Chihuahua, northern Sonora, and Baja California Norte. References are also made to Colorado, Utah, and Nevada.

Cell A small region of clear or pigmented membrane surrounded by the veins of an odonate's wing.

Cerci The pair of uppermost terminal abdominal appendages.

Compound eye An insect eye that's composed of a large number of smaller visual units.

Costa The thickened vein at the front (leading) edge of each wing. It may be a contrasting color. Approximately halfway out the wing, it is dented at the nodus.

Dorsal The top or upper surface.

Epiproct The lower terminal abdominal appendage of a dragonfly—used to clasp the female during copulation or while in tandem. Unlike in damselflies, this structure is unpaired.

Exuviae The last larval skin from which the adult odonate emerges. (Note: *exuvia* sometimes used as singular; *exuviae* often used as either singular or plural.)

Lateral On the side; i.e., stripes on the side of the thorax are lateral stripes.

Mesostigmal plates Low, sculptural ridges found on the upper surface of the prothorax of certain damselflies. During copulation or while in tandem, the male clasps these plates with his terminal abdominal segments. When viewed with magnification, they are valuable for identifying many female damselflies.

Nodus The approximate midpoint on the front edge of an odonate wing—may appear shallowly notched and have thickened veins or spots of color.

Obelisk position A behavioral means of staying cool; this posture is assumed by some dragonflies during hot weather—the abdomen is pointed skyward, decreasing the amount of solar radiation that strikes it.

Ocelli Three tiny light-sensing units situated atop the head near the antennae. The singular is *ocellus*.

Odonata The order—a taxonomic category—to which dragonflies and damselflies belong.

Odonate A member of the Odonata (sometimes shortened to "odes").

Oviposit The act of laying eggs.

Ovipositor The modified parts at the tip of a female odonate's abdomen with which she lays eggs.

Paraprocts The damselfly's lowermost pair of terminal abdominal appendages.

Prothorax The segment between the head and synthorax that bears the frontmost pair of legs. In many damselflies, this is where a male attaches himself to the female while copulating or in tandem. (In pond damselflies, the entire thorax is held by the male.)

Pruinescence The waxy white or pale blue deposit on a dragonfly's or damselfly's body or wings. The adjective is pruinose.

Shoulder stripe A dark line running diagonally from just above the base of the middle leg to the base of the front wing. Also called humeral stripe. May be uniform, split, constricted, or Y-shaped.

Stigma Greek for "spot." A specialized cell on the front edge and usually near the tip of an odonate wing. Elongated in some families. May be colored; rarely absent. Sometimes referred to as pseudostigma or pterostigma.

Stripes Markings that run lengthwise or top to bottom (but not side to side).

Synthorax Two fused body segments to which the second and third pairs of legs and the two pairs of wings are attached, as well as the abdomen and the prothorax. Also called pterothorax ("wing-thorax"), the attachment site of the wings.

Tandem The act of a male odonate clasping the female's head or thorax to hold her or to guard her from other males before, during, and/or after egg laying. Tandem pairs may be seen perched or in flight.

Teneral Odonata that have just emerged from their final larval skin. Typically, they are soft, pale colored, and fly weakly.

Terminal appendages The cerci, paraprocts, and epiprocts used by male Odonata to grasp the female during copulation, or while guarding her when in tandem. These are often important identification characteristics; in some families (such as darners) the female's appendages may also provide identification clues.

Thorax The combined prothorax and synthorax, the three segments that bear the wings and legs.

Ventral The lower surface or underside.

Zygoptera The suborder of the Odonata that contains the damselflies.

SUGGESTED READING AND USEFUL WEBSITES
••••••

Abbott, John C. *Dragonflies and Damselflies of Texas and the South-Central United States*. Princeton, NJ: Princeton University Press, 2005.

Biggs, Kathy. *Common Dragonflies of the Southwest: A Beginner's Pocket Guide*. Sebastopol, CA: Azalea Creek Publishing, 2004.

Dunkle, Sidney W. *Dragonflies through Binoculars: A Field Guide to Dragonflies of North America*. New York: Oxford University Press, 2000.

Manolis, Timothy D. *Dragonflies and Damselflies of California*. Berkeley, CA: University of California Press, 2003.

Mitchell, Forest L., and James L. Lasswell. *A Dazzle of Dragonflies*. College Station, TX: Texas A&M University Press, 2005.

Needham, James G., Minter J. Westfall Jr., and Michael L. May. *Dragonflies of North America*. Gainesville, FL: Scientific Publishers, 2000.

Nikula, Blair, Jackie Sones, and Donald and Lillian Stokes. *Stokes Beginner's Guide to Dragonflies*. New York: Little, Brown and Co., 2002.

Silsby, Jill. *Dragonflies of the World*. Washington, D.C.: Smithsonian Institution Press, 2001.

Westfall, Minter J. Jr., and Michael L. May. *Damselflies of North America*, 2nd ed. Gainesville, FL: Scientific Publishers, 2006.

Arizona Odonates, www.azodes.com/dragons/default.asp

California Dragonflies and Damselflies, www.sonic.net/dragonfly

CalOdes, http://groups.yahoo.com/group/CalOdes

OdonataCentral, www.odonatacentral.org

Odonata-L, https://mailweb.ups.edu/mailman/listinfo/odonata-l

Oregon Dragonfly and Damsel Survey, www.ent.orst.edu/ore_dfly

Dragonflies of New Mexico, www.rt66.com/~kjherman/odonata/NMdrgnfly.html

Slater Museum of Natural History (Includes many useful pages including an up-to-date list of North American species), www.ups.edu/x5666.xml

SoWestOdes, http://groups.yahoo.com/group/SoWestOdes

TexOdes, http://groups.yahoo.com/group/TexOdes

On Choosing Binoculars:

www.eagleoptics.com/index.asp?dept=1&type=12&pid=2417

www.naba.org/binocs.html

www.birds.cornell.edu/publications/livingbird/winter2005/age_binos.html

INDEX OF FEATURED SPECIES

· · · · · · ·

ACKNOWLEDGMENTS

• • • • • •

For providing expertise, enthusiasm, references, photos, unpublished records, and assistance with travel, and for reading portions of the manuscript and generally improving the quality of this book, thanks to: John C. Abbott, Lisa Anderson, Richard Bailowitz, Kathy and Dave Biggs, Hank and Priscilla Brodkin, Jerrell Daigle, Doug Danforth, Kim Davis, Sidney W. Dunkle, Peter J. Durkin, Richard Erickson, Ted L. Eubanks Jr., Rosser W. Garrison, Pete Haggard, Victor Harvey, Bob Honig, Ruth Hoyt, Marshall Iliff, Jim Johnson, Steve Krotzer, Robert R. Larsen, James Lasswell, Karen LeMay, Tim Manolis, Bill Mauffray, Forrest Mitchell, Dennis R. Paulson, Ryan Sawby, Bob Schiowitz, Karen Schober, Netta Smith, Mike Stangeland, Carrie Stusse, Sandy Upson, and Dale and Marian Zimmerman.